MW00849598

"Christian higher education has com[e] decision of which path to follow w[ith] direction of Christian educational ins[titutions] exhort and equip academic leaders to embrace and communicate a thorough (rather than a mere) Christian vision for their schools. Authors Scott Rae and Richard Langer are veteran educators and thus reliable guides for this journey. Highly recommended!"

—**Gregg R. Allison**, professor of Christian Theology,
The Southern Baptist Theological Seminary

"My longtime colleagues Rick Langer and Scott Rae have biblical integration skills on full display in this book. Some resources in Christian higher ed give generic education advice and slap some Christian language on it. Others are deeply Christian but lacking in a robust practical wisdom of how to apply those convictions. This has neither pitfall. It is rich in practical wisdom and profoundly Christian."

—**Barry H. Corey**, president, Biola University

"As Scott Rae and Rick Langer so clearly advocate, the unique mission of Christian universities is the flourishing of students, making them fully human by intentionally forming Christ followers who reflect Christlikeness. Rae and Langer contend that vocational calling plays a vital role in these institutions, from the board and president to new staff and professors. This is a must-read for anyone who cares deeply about the unique purposes and practice of Christian higher education at a time of so much swirl around its meaning and value."

—**Margaret Diddams**, editor, Christian Scholar's Review

"This mission-focused volume will enable board members, administrators, faculty, staff, students, parents, and donors to grasp the distinctive features of faithful Christ-centered education. Faculty members and administrators interested in the important connections between faith, teaching, learning, and living will want to reflect deeply on the wisdom offered in this significant work by these two thoughtful and seasoned educators. It is a genuine joy to recommend *Mission-Driven Colleges*, which offers much-needed guidance for the challenges facing Christian education, church, and culture today."

—**David S. Dockery**, president,
Southwestern Baptist Theological Seminary

"Contemporary higher education is frequently filled with rancor and divisiveness over its identity and purpose. Rae and Langer lucidly and persuasively paint an alternative portrait for what Christin universities can and should be, with clear mission rooted in a Christian view of reality with accompanying virtues and values. This is a must read for faculty, administrators and trustees as they seek 'to keep first things first' throughout their institution. A practical, powerful and significant contribution!"

—**Dennis Hollinger**, president emeritus & senior distinguished Professor of Christian Ethics, Gordon-Conwell Theological Seminary

"Next to the church, I believe Christian higher education is the hope of the world. Why? Because at its best, a truly Christian university shapes students who serve unselfishly out of a love for Jesus Christ at a cost to themselves. The world needs that kind of human being. Today we need more people shaped by a liberal arts curriculum that cultivates devoted hearts, courageous minds, and purposeful souls. Rae and Langer's book instructs people who care about American higher education on how to be the best, most effective version of themselves starting with understanding an institution's 'why.' An essential read for those leading in Christian higher education."

—**Shirley V. Hoogstra**, president, Council for Christian Colleges and Universities

"Our generation's most pressing questions revolve around identity, belonging, and purpose. How might we profit from asking the same questions of our institutions of Christian higher education? Answers and outcomes vary from one college to another. Not all universities that use 'Christian' as a descriptor reflect the same reasons for being. Not all share the same version and vision of human flourishing. Not all are in tune with their organizational sagas. Not all target learning beyond the immediate (and ever-evolving) job market. Not all are 'keeping first things first' as Christ-centered universities. In *Mission-Driven Colleges*, Rae and Langer lend important context and wise counsel for anyone with a stake in the perseverance of the Christian college enterprise. Prepare to be enlightened, encouraged, and equipped for lowering an anchor in the whitewater of Christian higher education."

—**Steven D. Mason**, president, LeTourneau University

"*Mission-Driven Colleges* is an essential guide for Christian educators committed to balancing the Christian faith and academic excellence. Langer and Rae bring the richness of decades of university teaching and biblical scholarship to addresses current realities within Christian higher education. Critiquing while never critical, they draw on a seminal and diverse set of sources to provide practical examples and generative questions. This leads to invaluable and practical insights in the integration of Christian mission to all aspects of university life. This book is surely a vital and indispensable resource for anyone committed to nurturing both faith and intellect in higher education."

—**Rob Rhea**, vice president of student life, Trinity Western University

MISSION-DRIVEN COLLEGES

Keeping First Things First
In Christian Higher Education

RICHARD LANGER AND SCOTT B. RAE

B&H
ACADEMIC®
BRENTWOOD, TENNESSEE

CONTENTS

FOREWORD

A colleague and I were recently talking about the lack of one specific resource in Christian higher education literature. Although the scholarship on faith and learning for faculty is fairly robust,[1] we lamented together that we need a book for new Christian college administrators and board members that could familiarize them with the basics of Christian higher education and the Christ-animating learning conversation. To my delight, *Mission-Driven Colleges: Keeping First Things First in Christian Higher Education* helpfully addresses some important aspects of this gap.

Scott Rae and Rick Langer have authored a book that is ideal for the novice administrator or board member who needs a primer on the important conversations in Christian higher education. Unfortunately, few Christian university development programs exist for new faculty administrators (e.g., vice presidents, deans, and chairs). For the programs that do exist and those that should be started, they should have the participants read this book. The particular reason for my assessment is that this book tackles the educational issues over which novice administrators and board members have the most control. They are the

---

[1] See, for example, the list of top Faith-Animating Learning books on the *Christian Scholar's Review* website, https://christianscholars.com/resources/top -faith-animating-learning-books/.

ones in charge of operationalizing the Christian mission by creating incentive systems for faculty.

Unfortunately, I usually see two problems with new Christian administrators or board members. First, they simply do not know the basic theological language of Christian higher education. Perhaps their own advanced education or business work has been guided largely by secular theories, frameworks, and ways of approaching the world. Thus, they do not even know the basics of how to think or speak theologically about the tasks they will be doing. Chapters 1 through 3 will help with those linguistic, theological, and theoretical competencies.

Second, I also find Christian administrators and board members who are fluent in Christian theological language but are limited in their application of it. They know how to talk about Christian higher education with clarity and sophistication. In fact, it is often clear that their vision for Christian higher education comes from their personally rich theological thinking and living. They are not like many of their peers in that they do not simply read the latest secular books on being a good chair, dean, vice president, provost, or president. They are experts at Christian rhetoric and even make strategic plans filled with Christian phrases and terminology. Yet they often still fail to provide clarity on how to operationalize this plan and move their rhetoric beyond catch-phrases such as the "integration of faith and learning" to help faculty on the ground who are moving from catchphrases to deeper understandings of God's world and wisdom.

It is because of this second problem that chapters 4 through 6 are so important. If Christian administrators do not know the first thing about crafting incentive structures for Christian faculty and staff or accountability mechanisms to make sure a Christian mission is fulfilled, they will ultimately fail to be excellent Christian administrators. Christ-animated administration requires knowledge, expertise, and wisdom that can only be learned from diving deep into the endeavor and being open to learning from experienced guides and mentors. Rae and Langer provide that guidance.

This book should only be the opening reading for any serious Christian administrator. In addition, the scholarship on Christ-animated learning, research, teaching, and administration has grown tremendously in the past three decades. This book should whet the reader's appetite for even further reading in this area. Indeed, Christian administrators and board members are shirking their duties if they do not move even deeper into their quest to be excellent administrators.

Perry L. Glanzer,
professor of educational foundations, Baylor University;
author of *Chrisitan Higher Education: An Empirical Guide* and
The Outrageous Idea of Christian Teaching

INTRODUCTION

Christian higher education can fail in either of two ways: by failing to be Christian or by failing to be higher education. This book is written to help Christian educators to succeed in both tasks.

The primary audience for this book is academic leaders: from the highest levels (boards and presidential cabinets), on down through provosts, deans, and department heads, and finally to faculty. Our Christian mission should guide academic research, the community life within our institutions, and our witness to the broader society. The structures that assure missional education takes place must address every aspect of university life. From top to bottom, our educational institutions must be structured to stimulate and sustain a distinctively Christian vision of all that the university exists to do.

Beyond the staff, faculty, and administrative leadership of a university, our book also addresses concerns that should be at the forefront of the minds of students and their parents as they make decisions about the school at which they want to pursue a Christian education. All Christian schools are not the same. Their values and intentions differ, even if they all share an overarching commitment to Christ.

I have heard parents explain that they chose a particular Christian university because it was "Christian enough" and the cost was substantially less than another Christian school that had a substantially greater emphasis on theology and Christian mission. This is a perfectly reasonable

choice—costs of higher education (Christian or otherwise) can be pro-
hibitive. But if one is making this choice, it is important to think carefully
about what would make an institution "Christian enough." Is it simply
having a Christian heritage? A denominational affiliation? A Bible class
required of each student? Service or chapel attendance requirements? It is
as important for parents and students to think carefully about Christian
higher education as it is for the leaders of Christian schools.

Making All Things Visible

One of the benefits of thinking carefully about our institutional mission
is that it helps us see what is otherwise invisible. Once we see clearly,
we are in a much better position to refine and improve the institutions
of which we are a part.

John Strassburger was the president of Ursinus College, a college
in Pennsylvania that had a deep missional commitment to liberal arts.
Unfortunately, "liberal arts" is a term that is commonly used but rarely
defined, so Ursinus embarked on a mission to define a liberal arts education and why it really mattered. It became clear that much of the
nature and many of the values of a liberal arts education went unappre-
ciated because they were not transparently obvious. One might say they
were hidden in plain sight. Strassburger goes on to explain:

> What our faculty members did was simple: They adopted a
> concept that was all the rage during the years that America was
> envying quality control in Japanese manufacturing. The Japanese
> word for it is "*mieruka*"—making all things visible. Our profes-
> sors set out to craft a set of programs that made all the virtues
> that we claim for liberal education clear and transparent.[1]

------

[1] John Strassburger, "For the Liberal Arts, Rhetoric Is Not Enough," *The
Chronicle of Higher Education*, February 28, 2010, https://www.chronicle.com/
article/for-the-liberal-arts-rhetoric-is-not-enough/.

Once the essential elements of a liberal arts education were made visible, the faculty at Ursinus structured them into a two-semester course known as the "Common Intellectual Experience," which was explicitly organized around helping students experience the value of an education that engaged the big questions of life. The same process led to restructuring summer school into one-on-one summer internships with students and faculty, and a variety of other changes. These highly successful transformations were the direct result of asking questions about the *telos*, or purpose/goal, of higher education. The question may have started as something abstract and philosophical, but caring enough about the questions allowed the university to operationalize the answers into the programs and curriculum that were transformative to the life of the university.

Imagine going through the same process to make visible the nature and value of Christian higher education. What is it that is different about Christian education from what is found in secular education, or liberal arts education, or professional education? Once those differences are understood, they can be made visible to all stakeholders within the community, they can be assessed in the educational curriculum, they can be used to market the institution to prospective students, they can be placed front and center in hiring decisions, and they can be used to motivate donors and to guide the board decisions.

Our Starting Point

This book was born of our own experience at trying to make all things visible. We have both spent decades working in Christian higher education, and we have each been directly involved in our institutional efforts at asking and answering the sorts of mission and vision questions that make up the heart of this book.

The framework of this book is drawn from a three-day Dean's Retreat that we facilitated in 2017. The purpose of the retreat was to clarify our vision of Christian education and deepen our ownership of our institutional mission at the level of the various schools that make up our university. Simply put, we wanted to make sure our efforts at Christian education were truly Christian and truly education.

The retreat was structured around in-depth conversations about four questions:

1. What is a university?
2. What is a Christian university?
3. What is *our* Christian university?
4. What is a Christian understanding of academic disciplines?

We strongly felt that only after these questions were answered could we as a university strategize, plan, and implement institutional structures for sustaining successful Christian higher education.

The retreat proved to be very valuable for our own institution. It was simple in structure but very meaningful. It was definitely time well spent for our own particular context, but we also realized that our format would apply with very minor changes to any other Christian school or university.

These framing questions appear to be simple. The simplicity makes one think the answers will be obvious and known to all, but in reality, the simplicity just means people tend to take the answers for granted. As one begins to discuss these questions, one quickly discovers that the answers are both complex and contested, but they are also essential for healthy institutional functioning.

These are not merely academic questions; they are institutional questions. The answers a college or university gives to these questions cannot be reduced to a statement on a website. Stated answers and real answers are two different things. Real answers are found in the actual practices that shape the university from top to bottom. They are embedded in institutional activity and cannot be reduced to institutional slogans. The primary task of the highest level of university leadership is to create structures that assure the ownership and implementation of the agreed-upon answers to these questions.

This book, then, is about **identifying, owning, and implementing the Christian mission of higher education in your particular school.** Our focus will be on the institutional questions that create the structure of the university. We will begin at the highest level of institutional mission and proceed toward increasingly specific levels and end just before the level of actual classroom instruction. It is at the level of the institution, not the classroom, that many of the most important questions of Christian higher education must be asked and answered.

We need both high-quality classroom-level integration and also high-quality institutional frameworks and commitments. We tend to write and think at the classroom level or at the theological/philosophical worldview level. What is much less common is to think of the *institutional* questions that must be answered in order to create and sustain faithful Christian instruction in the classroom. We must have both a clear vision of what a Christian vision for a university is, and a clear vision for how to communicate that vision within the curricular offerings that operationalize that mission.

This book will follow the structure we used for our deans retreat, and we hope it will generate equally fruitful dialogue in the academic communities of our readers. Chapter 1 addresses the question, "What is a university?" We recognize that the university today is vastly different from the traditional notion of the university when universities were founded. This chapter is purpose focused; it discusses questions such as "education for what purpose?" and "competence to what end?" The notion that higher education has a telos has become a quaint and outdated concept, but it is one that we believe must be resurrected if higher education is to become anything more than a very expensive way to ensure that graduates get jobs. Historically, education has been presumed to have some sort of social or moral purpose, yet much of higher education today regards those as either irrelevant or unresolvable, leaving the university with a nihilism regarding its purpose.

Chapter 2 becomes more specific, addressing the question, "What is a Christian university?" How is it different from the majority of colleges and universities that dot the landscape of higher education today? We will suggest that Christian universities are characterized by a distinctly Christian view of truth and knowledge that emerges from God's revelation both in his Word and his world. It is also characterized by a distinct view of what constitutes human flourishing (which is critically important to the task of higher education) and a Christian notion of calling and vocation.

Chapter 3 becomes even more specific, asking and answering the question, "What is *our* Christian university?" This chapter begins with the recognition that not all Christian universities are the same, nor do they have the same specific goals and values. It discusses the importance of knowing and preserving the "sacred core" of the institution, and thinking through how that unique, sacred core is expressed in all the facets of university life.

Chapter 4 considers the central role played by integration of faith and learning in any Christian university. Good integrative thinking ensures that the education that is delivered to students uses the lens of a distinctly Christian worldview. The general commitment to integration is widely accepted among Christian colleges and universities, but the definition of integration, the priority placed on it in the classroom, and how the goal of integration is executed in the curriculum varies widely among those who count integration as important. This chapter will attempt to answer the question, "What is a Christian academic discipline?" That is, what does a particular discipline look like through the framework of Christian faith? What does it mean for a psychologist to practice that discipline "Christianly"? What does Christian faith contribute to the study of sociology? How should faculty in the business school teach business and economics from within a biblical framework?

This chapter will look at some of the challenges that Christian colleges and universities face in doing integration well. We will suggest several indicators that integration is being taken seriously in the institution and will urge leadership to be consistent in its advertising of integration to potential students and their parents and the rigor with which integration is done in their curriculum.

Chapter 5 is specifically addressed to academic leadership in the Christian college and university setting—for department chairs, deans, provosts, and presidents. This chapter addresses how institutions can create and maintain a culture of missional fidelity, which very much includes how to cultivate and maintain an academic culture conducive to doing integration well. We are assuming that integration is indeed central to the institution's mission, but we recognize that mission faithfulness is not something that can be put on "automatic pilot." Both attention to mission and integration require constant vigilance, for without it, it is not difficult to experience mission drift, which, historically, has been more the norm than the exception for Christian schools.

Chapter 6 will end the book with a discussion that perhaps should have come at the beginning if we were to be true to the maxim, "Begin with the end in mind." This chapter addresses the question, "What is the Christian graduate?" That is, what kind of graduate do we want to produce at our institution? We recognize that we cannot accurately make this assessment until some years after graduation, but that is no excuse for failing to have a clear vision of what we are aiming for. In short, we want our graduates to be *faithful and flourishing disciples of Jesus*, with a faith that is deeply rooted, durable, and winsome. The goal is to lead a Christian university that is producing people who are truly faithful to the gospel and who preserve and proclaim the faith once for all delivered to the saints, but who are also addressing the real needs of the generation to which they have been called.

We are writing this book for those who want the "Christianness" of higher education to be a first thing, not an add-on or option. At every level, the goal of this book is to help us identify, own, and implement the mission of the university, then of the Christian university, then of our particular Christian university, and finally of the departments and disciplines that structure the university. Our hope is that every person who serves in a Christian university is able to understand how his or her job contributes to the success of a distinctively Christian educational mission. It is only through a united effort of all of our institutional resources that we will be able to produce the next generation of faithful followers of Jesus.

CHAPTER 1

WHAT IS A UNIVERSITY?

The fact is that too many young people attend college or
university, and their parents encourage them, without any
gripping sense of what college is all about beyond tentative
vocational goals or questionable social aspirations.[1]

Universities are among the most important institutions in modern cultures. They form our youth, preserve and impart human learning from previous generations, open pathways of service, develop transformational technologies, equip leaders of our society, and push forward the frontiers of human knowledge. But despite the unquestionable importance of universities, or perhaps because of it, stating their purpose is surprisingly difficult:

- Does a university exist to disseminate knowledge or to create it?
- Is a university intended to shape a person's soul or get a person a job?

---

[1] Arthur F. Holmes, *The Idea of a Christian College*, rev. ed. (Grand Rapids: Eerdmans, 1987), 3.

- Does a university serve the interests of the prevailing culture, or does it challenge and disrupt those interests?
- Is a university intended for the masses or the best and brightest?

These questions are not merely philosophical. Universities have limited resources and therefore need a well-defined mission and clear priorities to guide daily decisions on hiring, curriculum, recruitment of faculty and students, and raising funds. Moreover, the purpose of the university can be clearly seen in the questions asked when prospective students contemplate their higher education:

- Will my education get me a high-paying job?
- Will my education help me change the world?
- Will this college give me the best education and open doors for graduate school?
- Will my education help me find my purpose in life? my spouse? myself?
- Will my education help make me a better person and make my life more meaningful?

And, of course, parents, donors, and governments who fund education have their own versions of these questions. Asking, "What is a university for?" may sound philosophical, but it is among the most profound and practical questions facing higher education.

The University in Contemporary Culture

If one were to look carefully at the list of questions above, one would discover five basic conceptions of the telos of higher education hidden within them. These conceptions could be stated as follows:

1. Higher education for the sake of jobs
2. Higher education for the sake of justice
3. Higher education for the sake of knowledge (or truth)

4. Higher education for the sake of self-actualization

5. Higher education for the sake of human flourishing

Though we will consider each of these models shortly, it should be noted that these are not just fleeting notions that come to the minds of prospective college students in the early twenty-first century. These conceptions of a university have a long history. The academies of ancient Greece sought after truth and knowledge. At the same time, or perhaps at a deeper level, they thought the underlying purpose of an education was to make a certain kind of person—namely one who had the tools and character needed to govern themselves and their city well. One might see their conception of higher education as a hybrid of a truth and a human flourishing model. Medieval Christian universities shared a concern for truth and knowledge but also prepared students to serve in the learned vocations of medicine, law, and theology. Similarly, in 1635, Harvard was founded for a vocational purpose—assuring the new colonies would have educated ministers—but in the same period one finds the motto on the Harvard shield that bears the single word *Veritas*—Latin for "truth." A recent review article on European and American models of education identifies three nineteenth-century European models of education that match directly with the three models above: a German university model that seeks to advance knowledge, a French university model that is vocationally centered, and an Anglo-Saxon university model that focuses on human flourishing.[2] The article adds a fourth model associated with John Dewey in early twentieth-century America. This model is a hybrid of the other three models and adds a distinctively democratic and social element to education.

---

[2] Paul Ashwin, "The Educational Purposes of Higher Education: Changing Discussions of the Societal Outcomes of Educating Students," *Higher Education* 84, no. 6 (December 1, 2022): 1227–44, https://doi.org/10.1007/s10734-022-00930-9.

For some time, both insiders and those outside the university setting have raised questions about the telos (the intended end) of universities. As far back as the 1960s, University of California (UC) chancellor Clark Kerr began referring to the UC system as a "multi-versity" instead of a uni-versity, emphasizing the lack of a singular focus for university education. This is the point made in the early 1990s by the late social critic Neil Postman:

> Modern secular education is failing not because it doesn't teach who Ginger Rogers, Norman Mailer, and a thousand other people are but because it has no moral, social, or intellectual center. There is no set of ideas or attitudes that permeates all parts of the curriculum. The curriculum is not, in fact, a "course of study" but a meaningless hodgepodge of subjects. It does not even put forward a clear vision of what constitutes an educated person, unless it is a person who possesses "skills."[3]

Universities once existed not only to prepare people for their occupations, but they also took the moral formation of their students seriously. The goal was not only to produce productive graduates who would be good citizens, but also to produce morally good people. However, under the impact of moral relativism, there is no longer any unified concept of what constitutes a good person. Former Harvard president Derek Bok observes the following, "Relativism and individualism has rewritten the rules of the game; they have extinguished the motive for education."[4]

---

[3] Neil Postman, *Technolopy: The Surrender of Culture to Technology* (New York: Knopf, 1992), 185–86.

[4] Robert Fryling, "Campus Portrait," (address presented at National Staff Conference of InterVarsity Christian Fellowship, December 1992), cited in Stephen Garber, *The Fabric of Faithfulness: Weaving Together Belief and Behavior*, 2nd ed. (Downers Grove: IVP, 2007), 73.

Some years ago, then Chairman of the Securities and Exchange Commission John Shad gave Harvard Business School $30 million to establish a program in ethics. His good friend the late Chuck Colson pointedly told him that he was wasting his money because Harvard could not teach ethics. Shad challenged Colson to publicly tell that to the faculty and students at Harvard Business School—a challenge that Colson took up and repeated at most other Ivy League schools.[5] Colson later commented on how little critique he got from the students, which reinforced his point to Shad and reflects the relativism about which Bok spoke.

It appears, then, that we all agree that universities are extremely important, but, ironically, we have little or no consensus about what they are actually supposed to do. The university is an institution without a telos. Yuval Levin's book *A Time to Build* helps make sense of this swirling set of conceptions of a university.[6] As he surveys the controversies surrounding the university in the past two hundred years, he identifies three "cultures" within the modern university: professional training (vocation), activism and social change (justice), and liberal arts (human flourishing). Levin's specific insight is that *these cultures are usually all present within a single university*. Each of the three cultures believes it reflects the university's core ethic (what we have called telos), and each views the others as inadequate if not illegitimate. Champions of professional (pre-professional) development often implicitly regard both liberal education and moral activism as distractions from the practical aims of higher education. Champions of liberal education speak of both professional development and moral activism as profane intrusions

---

[5] To hear Colson's address at Harvard, see https://www.youtube.com /watch?v=HpHKWd0Wvo4.

[6] Yuval Levin, *A Time to Build: From Family and Community to Congress and the Campus, How Recommitting to Our Institutions Can Revive the American Dream* (New York: Basic Books, 2020).

into what should be an almost sacred realm reserved for the pursuit of truth, beauty, and goodness. Champions of moral activism treat both professional development and liberal education as callous and selfish—different forms of individual enrichment that would ignore the call of social justice. Levin describes the university that emerges from this contest of cultures as

> an institution largely directed at professional training, moved by an impulse for liberation from injustice, but always challenged by a small, persistent band of earnest and tradition-minded humanist gadflies. . . . We expect the university to take on a vast array of tasks, and we often find it embroiled in heated struggles to do so. *But these struggles are easier to understand when we see that they involve internal cultures at war over the soul of the institution, and when we see that they all have legitimate, longstanding claims.*[7]

Conceptions of the Modern University

For our purposes, we will return to the five different conceptions of the university mentioned at the outset of this section but keep Levin's insight regarding internal factions clearly in mind. Those who are guiding a university need to understand what the university is there to do—what conception of the university is primary. At the same time, they must acknowledge the presence of other conceptions that are almost certainly present within the faculty, staff, and student body. A certain amount of ambiguity concerning the telos of the university is to be expected and in all likelihood contributes vital energy to the life of the university. It is important, however, that those in leadership can identify and clearly state the guiding purpose of their institution. If conflicting

---

[7] Levin, 98. Emphasis added.

cultures simply wrangle with each other in a free market within a single institution, an incoherent vision will result in the minds of university stakeholders making effective leadership nearly impossible. Let us think more closely about each of these models.

Higher education for the sake of jobs

This telos is neither as cynical nor as modern as it may sound. In their medieval origins, Western universities trained students for the three "learned professions": theology, medicine, and law. Since the 1860s in America, land grant institutions have emerged as a robust form of the university. Originally, they were explicitly focused on agriculture and the mechanical arts rather than liberal arts (hence the A&M in the name of many of these universities). As the years have gone by, these universities have developed robust liberal arts programs, but that has never displaced the vocational focus, which has continued to expand. As a result, it is not uncommon to find under the umbrella of a single university a teaching college, a fine arts school, a business school, a film school, an engineering school, an agricultural school, and, of course, schools of the traditional medieval vocations of theology, law, and medicine.

Equally important is the fact that incoming students are seeking a job. In 1969, approximately 45 percent of college freshman identified becoming financially well off as either essential or very important to their decision to go to college. In 2019, that number had risen to 85 percent—the highest percentage of the twenty items rated in the survey.[8] Similar results are found when surveying college graduates about what they were seeking when they enrolled. Alumni indicated they were hoping to qualify for good jobs (87 percent), to gain skills to be successful

---

[8] "The American Freshman: National Norms Fall 2019," Higher Education Research Institute, accessed June 23, 2023, https://www.heri.ucla.edu/monographs/TheAmericanFreshman2019.pdf.

in work (86 percent), and to advance their careers (84 percent). Slightly less prevalent were goals related directly to income: to be able to support myself and my family (82 percent) and to make more money (72 percent).[9] Equally indicative of the job-centric telos of higher education is the choice of majors. The five most common undergraduate majors in 2018, in descending order of popularity, were business, nursing, psychology, biology (including pre-medicine), and engineering—all of which suggest a vocational orientation among students.[10]

Nonetheless, education for the sake of a job is clearly in tension with liberal arts education. As the statistics show, students want jobs, and not just because meaningful work contributes to human flourishing or meaning in life or some other humanistic goal. Rather, students attend college to get a better *paying* job—they are hoping for a good economic return on investment. In fact, the Georgetown University Center for Education and the Workforce (CEW) has begun ranking 4,500 post-secondary schools in the United States according to their return on investment.[11] Their research confirms the economic benefit of a degree when viewed over a forty-year working lifetime, but the methodology of the rankings reveals a troubling assumption. The rankings weigh increased earnings from paid employment, against the cost of the education: tuition, room, and board. This much seems obvious. But the costs do not end there. Since a student is assumed to be out of the workforce while in school, the rankings deduct lost wages that could have been earned if one was working instead of studying. The methodological assumption is that there is no *intrinsic* value to an education. Education is assessed as "lost time." It

[9] "Student Outcomes Beyond Completion: National Findings from the 2021 Strada Alumni Survey," Strada, accessed June 6, 2023, https://cci.stradaeducation.org/pv-release-oct-27-2021/.

[10] Levin, *A Time to Build*, 93.

[11] "Ranking 4,500 Colleges by ROI (2022)," *Georgetown University Center for Education and the Workforce* (blog), accessed June 22, 2023, https://cew.georgetown.edu/cew-reports/roi2022/.

is mistaken to assume that neither those who do the rankings nor students who might use them care about human flourishing or other intrinsic values of education. However, there is simply no place for including soft (noneconomic) values like human flourishing in the ranking. This sort of assessment of education calls to mind a 1968 speech given by Robert F. Kennedy at the University of Kansas:

> Yet the gross national product does not allow for the health of our children, the quality of their education or the joy of their play. It does not include the beauty of our poetry or the strength of our marriages, the intelligence of our public debate or the integrity of our public officials. It measures neither our wit nor our courage, neither our wisdom nor our learning, neither our compassion nor our devotion to our country, *it measures everything in short, except that which makes life worthwhile.* And it can tell us everything about America except why we are proud that we are Americans.[12]

Kennedy cautions his hearers to think carefully about what they are counting. He warns against a society that loses sight of noneconomic values such as poetry, intelligent debate, integrity, wit, and courage as well as compassion and devotion to our country. He commends the university as a place where such values could be cultivated. C. S. Lewis offers a similar critique when he suggests that it is exactly *not* our professions that make us human:

> That is why education seems to me so important: it actualizes that potentiality for leisure, if you like for amateurishness, which is man's prerogative . . . man is the only amateur animal;

---

[12] "Remarks at the University of Kansas, March 18, 1968," John F. Kennedy Presidential Library and Museum, accessed June 25, 2023, https://www.jfklibrary .org/learn/about-jfk/the-kennedy-family/robert-f-kennedy/robert-f-kennedy -speeches/remarks-at-the-university-of-kansas-march-18-1968. Emphasis added.

all the others are professionals. They have no leisure and do not desire it. When the cow has finished eating she chews the cud; when she has finished chewing she sleeps; when she has finished sleeping she eats again. She is a machine for turning grass into calves and milk. . . . The lion cannot stop hunting, nor the beaver building dams, nor the bee making honey. When God made the beasts dumb, He saved the world from infinite boredom, for if they could speak they would all of them, all day, talk nothing but shop.[13]

Arthur Holmes likewise states that "liberal learning concerns itself with truth and beauty and goodness, which have intrinsic worth to people considered as persons rather than as workers or in whatever function alone."[14]

The bottom line is that there is no avoiding the connection between jobs and education, and providing education for professional service is a long-standing function of the university. However, a university that conceives of itself exclusively or primarily as a job-training institution has chosen a telos that fails to account for some of the most fundamental goods of an education and is also in danger of subordinating its mission to serving business and the economy rather than truth, knowledge, or human flourishing. These concerns should be sufficient to make one, at the very least, consider alternatives.

Higher education for the sake of justice

Social activism has always been a part of university life. William Allen White, a renowned journalist and politician of the early twentieth century, commented on student unrest in his day, saying that

---

[13] C. S. Lewis, *Rehabilitations and Other Essays* (Folcroft, PA: Folcroft Library Editions, 1973), 81.

[14] Holmes, *The Idea of a Christian College*, 28.

student riots of one sort or another . . . indicate a healthy growth and a normal functioning of the academic mind. Youth should be radical. Youth should demand change in the world. Youth should not accept the old order if the world is to move on. But the old orders should not be moved easily. . . . There must be clash and if youth hasn't enough force or fervor to produce the clash the world grows stale and stagnant and sour in decay. If our colleges and universities do not breed men who riot, who rebel, who attack life with all the youthful vim and vigor, then there is something wrong with our colleges. The more riots that come on college campuses, the better world for tomorrow.[15]

White's comments are intentionally provocative, but he makes a valid point: student activism is nothing new. Even premodern university students were organizing protests—sometimes regarding their own living conditions, and sometimes regarding larger civic or political concerns. In the United States, student activism has addressed a host of causes from poor living conditions, to fear of being drafted into the military, to slavery, civil rights, war, and inequality.[16] Today, many universities explicitly acknowledge social activism in their institutional documents, websites, and marketing materials. Regis University, a Catholic university in Denver, states that "a Jesuit education is all about social justice, equality and development of the whole person."[17] Wesleyan University wants to be recognized for offering "a creative, rigorous, pragmatic liberal education that fosters personal development and social responsibility

---

[15] William Allen White, "Student Riots," *Emporia Gazette*, April 8, 1932, https://www.bartleby.com/lit-hub/respectfully-quoted/william-allen-white -18681944/.

[16] Levin, *A Time to Build*, 95.

[17] Dave Francois, "Higher Education, Higher Calling," Regis University, January 6, 2021, https://www.regis.edu/news/2021/discern-learn/01/what-is -jesuit-education.

while empowering graduates to shape a changing world."[18] Harvard University boasts that it offers an education that will "unsettle presumptions, to defamiliarize the familiar, to reveal what is going on beneath and behind appearances, to disorient young people and to help them to find ways to re-orient themselves . . . [and to expose] them to the sense of alienation produced by encounters with radically different historical moments and cultural formations."[19]

Social activism is not just the domain of "woke" universities. Christian universities often include activism as part of their mission—even if their activist vision points in a different direction. Our own school (Biola University) seeks to graduate students who will "impact the world for Jesus Christ." Countless other evangelical schools include similar language in their mission statements. Christians may talk about changing the world from the inside out, or from the bottom up, or one person at a time, but changing the world from the bottom up or the top down is a debate about means and not about ends. If you are planning on changing the world, you are, by definition, an activist.

Universities across the spectrum care about social action; however, it is less clear that this can serve as the defining telos of a university. Jonathan Haidt, a professor at New York University and a founder of the Heterodox Academy, distinguishes "two incompatible sacred values" of the university—social justice and truth—and he identifies a patron saint for each:

> *"The philosophers have only interpreted the world, in various ways; the point is to change it."* —Karl Marx, 1845

---

[18] "Towards Wesleyan's Bicentennial," Wesleyan University, accessed January 25, 2023, https://www.wesleyan.edu/strategicplan/index.html#mission.

[19] *Report of the Task Force on General Education* (The President and Fellows of Harvard College, February 2007), 1–2, https://projects.iq.harvard.edu/files /gened/files/genedtaskforcereport.pdf?m=1448033208.

"He who knows only his own side of the case knows little of that. His reasons may be good, and no one may have been able to refute them. But if he is equally unable to refute the reasons on the opposite side, if he does not so much as know what they are, he has no ground for preferring either opinion." —John Stuart Mill, 1859

Marx is the patron saint of what I'll call "Social Justice U," which is oriented around changing the world in part by overthrowing power structures and privilege. It sees political diversity as an obstacle to action. Mill is the patron saint of what I'll call "Truth U," which sees truth as a process in which flawed individuals challenge each other's biased and incomplete reasoning. In the process, all become smarter. Truth U dies when it becomes intellectually uniform or politically orthodox.[20]

Haidt argues that truth and social justice cannot both serve as "sacred values" because they point the university in different directions. Social activism needs political orthodoxy and intellectual uniformity, while truth needs a diversity of opinions that face continual testing and competition. Haidt is concerned not so much with the activism of individual students or groups of students who might share a common cause. This is nothing new. Rather, he is concerned about institutional activism—social justice that is owned by the institution, that uses the institution as a pulpit or platform, that enforces its orthodoxy in hiring practices and expresses it in speech codes and curricular requirements. That is something both new and problematic in Haidt's mind. He does not want social justice institutions to be forbidden; rather, he wants them to clearly label and communicate their chosen telos, because it

---

[20] Jonathan Haidt, "Why Universities Must Choose One Telos: Truth or Social Justice," *Diverse Perspectives: The HxA Blog*, Heterodox Academy, October 22, 2016, https://heterodoxacademy.org/blog/one-telos-truth-or-social-justice-2/.

departs from what he understands the long-standing telos of the university to be.

Haidt is right in asking university leadership to clearly identify the university telos. The defining telos is not the exclusive purpose of the university, but it is the organizing purpose. The education for the sake of justice, just like education for the sake of a job, is organized around something that is highly valued by our society, that is long associated with the university (at least in Western cultures), and that almost every university would deem to be important. The question is whether these values should serve as the defining telos for the university, or as purposes subordinated to some other telos. Social justice, on the surface, seems to be a political task that might better serve as the defining telos of government or social and political action organizations rather than an educational institution. Education can be used to serve social justice, just as it can be used to get a job, but the connection appears to be instrumental rather than intrinsic. Education seems to be intrinsically associated with the life of the mind, and hence Haidt suggests truth as a better telos.

Higher education for the sake of knowledge

"Truth U" is Haidt's way of identifying what we are calling "education for the sake of knowledge." It seeks to make the university a community of free inquiry because free inquiry is the only way to find truth. If our ideas are not tested, individuals will fall prey to their own confirmation bias and end up missing the mark when it comes to truth. Many American educators have identified truth—or, more commonly, knowledge—as the defining purpose of the university. For example, Daniel Coit Gilman, the first president of Johns Hopkins, said that "[the university] renders services to the community which . . . no mathematical process [could] ever compute. These functions may be stated as the acquisition, conservation, refinement, and distribution of knowledge."[21] The Yale Woodward Report simply stated that "the primary function of a university is to discover and disseminate knowledge by means of research and teaching."[22]

It is natural to wonder, however, if the discovery and dissemination of knowledge is expansive enough to cover all higher education. Do we not want an education to make better people, not just more informed people or people with better academic skills? Some may feel this way, but Stanley Fish, a scholar and administrator at Duke University, strenuously objects to education that drifts away from a narrowly defined academic task. Attempts to form character and address the big questions of life go beyond what can reasonably be expected of an education, he writes, noting that

> you can reasonably set out to put your students in possession of a set of materials and equip them with a set of skills . . . and even perhaps (although this one is really iffy) instill in them the same love of the subject that inspires your pedagogical efforts. . . . And you have no chance at all (short of a discipleship that is itself suspect and dangerous) of determining what their behavior and values will be in those aspects of their lives that are not, in the strict sense of the word, academic. You might just make them into good researchers. You can't make them into good people, and you shouldn't try.[23]

---

[21] Daniel Coit Gilman, *University Problems in the United States* (New York: Arno Press, 1969), 55, http://archive.org/details/universityprobl00gilmgoog.

[22] "Report of the Committee on Freedom of Expression at Yale," Yale College, December 23, 1974, https://yalecollege.yale.edu/get-know-yale-college/office-dean/reports/report-committee-freedom-expression-yale.

[23] Stanley Eugene Fish, *Save the World on Your Own Time* (New York: Oxford University Press, 2008), 58–59.

For Stanley Fish, college education is cognitive and academic. It might cultivate love for a particular subject, but it cannot succeed in creating well-ordered sentiments in the soul. It cannot cultivate personal morality or virtuous character, and it should not try. Those things are going to have to happen on someone else's time. Part of why Fish had to write his book, however, is that so many people see things otherwise.

Those who disagree with Fish (and perhaps Haidt and Gilman as well) point out that knowledge is often valued instrumentally—it is good when it is good for something. Knowledge is meant to be used. This is a debatable point, and for many people, the force of this argument could be blunted if one talks about truth instead of knowledge. Truth is one of the transcendentals—truth, beauty, and goodness—and the transcendentals are to be valued for their own sake. But then we must ask if truth alone can serve as the telos of a university. Can we afford to pursue truth and do without beauty and goodness? Can beauty and goodness be subsumed under truth? It is not obvious that the answer to either of these questions is yes. Traditional liberal education is pursued for its own sake, but it has never focused exclusively on a narrowly academic and modern conception of truth. It has also sought to cultivate less tangible qualities of the soul, including the very things Fish dismisses from the educational project.

A friend of mine attended a panel discussion on the liberal arts at an Ivy League school. During the question-and-answer time, a student in the audience expressed his awe at a recent scientific discovery that could potentially restore sight to a blind person. He then asked why he should be required to study the humanities when it is science that can make blind people see. One of the panelists said, "So that a such a person has something worth seeing." That is a good response. Discovering scientific truths is important, but so is cultivating and curating that which is good, beautiful, and worth seeing.

Furthermore, pursuing knowledge sounds pure and high-minded, but as Francis Bacon pointed out, knowledge is power. Education for the sake of knowledge can easily become education for the sake of power. This sort of university exists to discover knowledge and use it for power over nature and over other people. C. S. Lewis warned of this dangerous aspect of the modern impulse to conquer nature and subordinate it to our own purposes, observing that

> there is something which unites magic and applied science while separating both from the "wisdom" of earlier ages. For the wise men of old the cardinal problem had been how to conform the soul to reality, and the solution had been knowledge, self-discipline, and virtue. For magic and applied science alike the problem is how to subdue reality to the wishes of men: the solution is a technique; and both, in the practice of this technique, are ready to do things hitherto regarded as disgusting and impious.[24]

The foresight of Lewis's analysis and the legitimacy of his fears have only increased in the intervening decades. Artificial intelligence, gene manipulation, and transhumanism have moved from the pages of science fiction novels to the headlines of our newspapers. This has happened not because of evil people intending to harm others but because of clever people discovering truth without considering the uses to which those truths might be put. The essayist, novelist, poet, and public intellectual Wendell Berry feels the university is obliged to know and care how truth is used:

> If, for the sake of its own health, a university must be interested in the question of the truth of what it teaches, then, for the sake of the world's health, it must be interested in the fate of that

---

[24] C. S. Lewis, *The Abolition of Man, Or, Reflections on Education with Special Reference to the Teaching of English in the Upper Forms of Schools* (Springfield, OH: Collier Books, 1986), 87–88.

truth and the uses made of it in the world. It must want to know where its graduates live, where they work, and what they do.[25]

Truth, therefore, is a necessary part of education, but it cannot serve as the exclusive goal—at least not when it is narrowly defined. Truth stands in relation to other necessary goods, and when those are neglected, the university can be impaired in its effectiveness or even become harmful to the larger society. As Lewis states, it is dangerous when the ancient wisdom of conforming a soul to reality has been neglected or lost completely in a rush to find new truth, new technologies, and greater power. Lewis and Berry both concern themselves with preserving ancient truths, which contain hard-won lessons about the nature of humanity and the relationship between humanity and the world in which we live. But before we look deeper into these permanent truths, we need to consider an alternative vision of human flourishing and liberal education.

Higher education for the sake of self-actualization

Education for the sake of self-actualization sounds decidedly modern, and in many ways it is—the language of self-actualization was practically unknown before 1960. Nonetheless, it draws from a deep well. In some ways, it is simply a modern conception of human flourishing. In previous eras, it was assumed that there was some external reality that provided a standard of human flourishing to which a person was supposed to conform his or her soul. One can see this viewpoint in the quote from C. S. Lewis above when he describes wisdom as learning to conform one's soul to reality. That reality might be grounded in God, or in the Platonic form of the human, or simply in an objectively existing human nature, but wherever it

---

[25] Wendell Berry and Jacques Maritain, *The Loss of the University* (Washington, DC: The Trinity Forum, 2022), 21.

is grounded, that place is *external* to the individual. The modern twist is to individualize human nature, to personalize it, or to simply declare that there is no human nature other than what any individual human being deems to be natural for themselves. Flourishing in such a case involves a process of self-discovery, self-actualization, and self-expression, the end result of which is personal authenticity. It is not a matter of training students to be citizens of a democracy or shaping students according to an independent and preexisting human nature or imparting to students the intellectual inheritance of previous generations. Instead, education is the rain and sunshine that lets students blossom into all they were meant to be.

This sort of expressive individualism has been described in depth by scholars such as Robert Bellah and Charles Taylor.[26] Taylor sees the modern preoccupation with self-expression as part of a broader culture of authenticity that claims "*each one of us has his/her own way of realizing our humanity*, and that it is important to find and live out one's own, as against surrendering to conformity with a model imposed on us from outside, by society, or the previous generation, or religious or political authority."[27] Taylor describes a sort of self-expressive individualism that might be read as an homage to U.S. Supreme Court Justice Anthony Kennedy's words in the Casey decision: "At the heart of liberty is the right to define one's own concept of existence, of meaning, of the universe, and of the mystery of human life."[28] In fact, the authenticity culture within education dates back to Jean-Jacques Rousseau, a leading figure in eighteenth-century Romanticism, who was deeply skeptical of the influence of society in education, and simultaneously optimistic about the native abilities of students. For him, education should be

---

[26] Robert Neelly Bellah, *Habits of the Heart: Individualism and Commitment in American Life* (Berkeley: University of California Press, 1985); Charles Taylor, *A Secular Age* (Cambridge, MA: Harvard University Press, 2007).

[27] Taylor, *A Secular Age*, 475. Emphasis added.

[28] Planned Parenthood v. Casey, 505 U.S. 833 (Supreme Court, June 29, 1992).

discovering truth on one's own, not learning truth from others. Learning from others is just "time lost in learning to think for ourselves, we have more acquired knowledge and less vigor of mind. Our minds like our arms are accustomed to use tools for everything, and to do nothing for themselves."[29]

One way to identify a university culture that is shaped by expressive individualism is to ask if the curriculum is formed by the university faculty or by the individual student. Is there a core of received wisdom that the university deems necessary for a person to be considered well educated, or is the curriculum designed by appeal to the interests and values of the students themselves with little regard to the surrounding culture or the intellectual legacy of previous generations? An example of this student-centered approach can be found in Brown University's description of their "open curriculum":

> At most universities, students must complete a set of core courses. At Brown, our students develop a personalized course of study. . . . Brown's distinctive approach asks much of students—*as the architect of their own education, Brown students are responsible for their own intellectual and creative development.*[30]

Education for self-actualization is not confined to the academic curriculum. Students who are seeking a job will often be guided to career centers that focus their efforts on self-discovery and identity formation. Psychological assessments are mapped onto jobs that are likely to be fulfilling to the unique strengths, abilities, and personality type of the individual student. Social activism can also be a great vehicle for

---

[29] Jean-Jacques Rousseau, *Emile: or on Education*, ed. Barbara Foxley (North Chelmsford, MA: Courier Corporation, 2013), 369.

[30] "The Open Curriculum," Brown University, accessed October 25, 2022, https://www.brown.edu/academics/undergraduate/open-curriculum. Emphasis added.

self-expression by tapping into a student's passions. What is distinctive about education for self-actualization of the student is that it organizes the institutional structures around empowerment of the individual students as they are—a university education is not viewed as a project of self-improvement that makes a better person; it is a project of self-expression that energizes and empowers what the student brings to the table to begin with.

The downside to education for self-actualization is partly pragmatic. The demands placed on budget, staffing, and academic programs are substantial. Universities cannot multiply majors and specialized services without compromising other aspects of the university. Nor is it clear that the university is a cost-effective place to engage in a project of self-discovery and identity formation. It is beyond question that this sort of personal growth is a central part of late adolescence, and as a result, it will always be part of college life. The question is whether this can serve as the defining telos of a university.

Beyond pragmatic concerns, there is an intrinsic paradox built into these views of the student. Are incoming students mature human beings who can architect their own education, or are they people who are just beginning to form their own identities? Do incoming student know where they are going in life, or do they need help to navigate the perplexing challenges of transitioning from adolescence to adulthood? Do students need instruction, direction, and guidance, or do they just need the freedom and empowerment to be the person they already are? Is an eighteen-year-old who is struggling with his or her own identity ready to be empowered for social activism intended to reshape society as a whole? Speaking at his own commencement, a Harvard graduate described his education experience as long on freedom but short on direction.

> They tell us that it is heresy to suggest the superiority of some value, fantasy to believe in moral argument, slavery to submit to a judgment sounder than your own. The freedom of our day is

the freedom to devote ourselves to any values we please, on the mere condition that we do not believe them to be true.[31]

Every institution of higher education must be guided by a clear understanding of what their incoming students are like and hence what they need to gain in their four years of education. Harry Lewis, former professor and dean at Harvard University, is deeply concerned that we misunderstand student needs and that many educators

> have forgotten that the fundamental job of undergraduate education is to turn eighteen- and nineteen-year-olds into twenty-one- and twenty-two-year-olds, to help them grow up, to learn who they are, to search for a larger purpose for their lives, and to leave college as better human beings.[32]

It would appear, then, that it is problematic to assume that all one needs to give incoming freshman is the freedom to discover themselves. In fact, it is natural to assume that part of the function of education is helping students discover, understand, and appreciate truths anchored in something outside of just themselves.

Higher education for the sake of human flourishing

Education for the sake of human flourishing is distinct from education for the sake of self-actualization in that it assumes there is such a thing as human nature that can sit in judgment upon the desires of a particular human being. A clear understanding of human nature can help a person discern if a particular object of desire is in fact desirable, or whether a person has mistakenly desired something that is

---

[31] Robert Bellah et al., *The Good Society* (New York: Knopf Doubleday, 2011), 44.
[32] Harry Lewis, *Excellence Without a Soul: Does Liberal Education Have a Future?* (New York: PublicAffairs, 2007), xii.

destructive and detrimental to human flourishing. In this view, human nature is a real thing with a particular telos that does not fundamentally change as individuals, nations, empires, and entire cultures come and go. Therefore, it is natural and expected that higher education imparts the wisdom of previous generations. There are things about being human that transcend our particularity and endure through the ages. Anthony Kronman, former dean of Yale Law School, writes that there are

> facts of life we all confront and have no choice but to accept . . . [that] we all die and we know we will . . . that we all hunger for love and recognition and a satisfying connection with others . . . that we are limited and yet relatively equal in our powers, so that cooperation among us is both possible and required; that we create laws and live in political communities; that we take pleasure in knowledge for its own sake.[33]

Not all thinkers use the same language to discuss human flourishing. Kronman focuses on the big questions of the meaning of life. The Catholic philosopher Alasdair MacIntyre suggests that we must determine what it is to be a human being.[34] Wendell Berry argues that "the thing being made in a university is humanity . . . not just trained workers or knowledgeable citizens but responsible heirs and members of human culture."[35] Some universities base their curriculum on the "transcendentals"—truth, beauty, and goodness—or on great books to bring the enduring questions of human life to the fore. Regardless of the exact language, the unifying telos is imparting wisdom about the

---

[33] Anthony T. Kronman, *Education's End: Why Our Colleges and Universities Have Given Up on the Meaning of Life* (New Haven, CT: Yale University Press, 2008), 76–77.

[34] Alasdair MacIntyre, *God, Philosophy, Universities: A Selective History of the Catholic Philosophical Tradition* (Lanham, MD: Rowman & Littlefield, 2011), 177.

[35] Berry and Maritain, *The Loss of the University*, 14.

permanent things that contribute to the flourishing of a real human nature. This does not entail a narrow agreement on a single viewpoint. All that is required is that there is such a thing as human life and that no matter when and where it is lived, a human life confronts one with a set of transcendently important questions that must be answered. A good education makes a student conversant with these questions and equipped to engage them not only while at the university but throughout the course of their life.

The organizing telos of human flourishing does not preclude the other cultures of the university. Finding a job, working for justice, discovering truth, and becoming who you were meant to be are not excluded by affirming there is a universal human nature. In fact, one might argue that these other pursuits emerge from the very features of our shared human nature. Human flourishing does not ignore jobs, it requires jobs. But it also changes one's perspective on jobs, viewing jobs as an aspect of something more transcendent, like a notion of calling that is essential to human flourishing. It would also place work in relation to other human goods such as family, leisure, and worship. Likewise, it does not discount the importance of social activism, but it will focus more deeply on the nature of justice (and how it differs from freedom and equality) and seek to understand how these and other social virtues contribute to a flourishing human society. It regards truth highly, but also asks what is to be done with truth and how truth stands in relation to beauty and goodness and to faith and hope and love. Finally, it does not diminish the dignity and significance of the individual, but it asks for critical self-knowledge and sober reflection on one's desires before deciding whether one's desires are worthy of seeking self-expression. Human flourishing sees the wisdom of previous generations not merely as opinions of bygone generations but as a cultural inheritance essential to the flourishing of both individuals and society as a whole.

Of course, education for human flourishing must address its own problems. A common critique of education for human flourishing is that it can easily confuse the values of a particular time or place with permanent things and transcendent values. What counts as a great book or one of life's big questions can vary from culture to culture—and it is not easy to identify virtues, or ideas, or desires, or social structures that do not. There may be a blurred line between an education based on the transcendentals and simply practicing a sophisticated version of imperialism and ethnocentrism. Also, the criticism of Stanley Fish about the difficulty of making good people may be overstated, but it is certainly difficult to guarantee that a student is formed into a good person, and it may be hard to demonstrate that a university education succeeds in making students "more fully human." And finally, the humanities do not pay the light bills at modern universities, and practical realities of finances and student enrollment cannot be ignored at any time—particularly not in the current context when demographics and inherent costs of higher education are creating powerful headwinds.

Conclusion

This chapter is meant to help the reader think carefully and clearly about the telos of the university. It is also meant to provide a vocabulary and conceptual categories for understanding the internal and external conflicts that permeate the modern university. Five different conceptions of the defining purpose of the university were identified, and each was associated with a university "culture" that can lay claim to a relatively long-standing tradition. Each of these conceptions of the university has broad enough appeal to attract a sufficient number of students and donors to keep a university running. Furthermore, a university can organize around any one of these cultures and still meet credentialing standards that allow for their degrees to be recognized by other universities as well as businesses, professional societies, and governmental agencies. Any of these conceptions can be connected to the Christian faith, but the deepest and most natural connections are likely to emerge from higher education for the sake of human flourishing, though that is a question that requires a much more extended discussion.

Questions

1. Identify ways in which the five conceptions of higher education are found at your own institution. Which vision is most dominant? What are some tensions between these conceptions?

2. Identify particular statements, practices, and structures that you believe are meant to express the chosen telos (purpose) of your institution. How effective are they in clarifying your institution's purpose to students, faculty, and staff? (If you are drawing a blank, consider things like commonly repeated phrases from a mission statement, course requirements for all students, chapel programs, student service requirements, or the qualities that are honored or celebrated in your alumni.)

3. If you were to look at official documents, the website, and official magazines, newsletters, or other forms of communication, what would you identify as the guiding purpose of your institution?

CHAPTER 2

WHAT IS A CHRISTIAN UNIVERSITY?

Christian perspectives can generate a worldview large
enough to give meaning to all the disciplines and delights
of life and to the whole of a liberal education.[1]

Why do we need Christian universities and not just secular universities? This sounds like a reasonable question, but historically, it is exactly the wrong question to ask. In the Western world, higher education began almost nine hundred years ago with church-related universities in cities like Bologna, Oxford, and Cambridge. Similar universities arose across Europe, almost always in affiliation with either Catholic or Protestant churches and religious orders. In North America, the earliest universities like Harvard, Yale, William & Mary, and Princeton were affiliated with Christian denominations, founded with the purpose of assuring an educated clergy. As

---

[1] Arthur F. Holmes, *The Idea of a Christian College*, rev. ed. (Grand Rapids: Eerdmans, 1987)

late as 1951, half of all college students in the United States were still being educated in private universities, the vast majority of which were founded as church-related institutions. Christian higher education is not a *stepchild* of secular higher education; it is the *seedbed* from which the secular educational system was born.

One could, however, argue that while the Christian faith served as the seedbed of the university, that time is long past. Is there still a need for a Christian university? Perhaps the church spawning the university was a historical accident. The church met a need for education when no other part of society was organized to do so. In the present day, however, our government is (arguably) capable of meeting this need. If there is no intrinsic need for Christian education, and if there is nothing unique about Christian education, then perhaps it is all right for Christian universities to fade away and allow the government or private secular universities to take over the task of higher education.

In the past few centuries, many Christian thinkers have considered questions like these, and few have spoken more clearly and comprehensively than Abraham Kuyper. Kuyper was a leading figure in the Netherlands in the late nineteenth and early twentieth centuries. He was a pastor, a journalist, a theologian, and the founder of a political party. He even served as prime minister of the Netherlands for a term. He was also very deeply engaged in Christian education, both as a scholar and as a founder of the Free University of Amsterdam. Kuyper thought carefully about Christianity and human society. He argued that society needs to be ordered around certain spheres of life that are built into the creation order—spheres such as the family, the church, the government, and education. Each of these spheres has its own sacred trust; each has its own sphere of life over which it is sovereign in the sense that it answers to God rather than some other human authority. Educational institutions exercise their sphere of sovereignty over learning and disseminating truth to the rest of society. But if this task defines all education, what is unique to Christian education? According to Kuyper, it is the person of Christ himself. Kuyper's thought on this matter is worth quoting at length.

> What, you may ask, has the plant kingdom, for example, to do with Christ? Those who ask this question are answered that the Christ is the eternal Word, and that through this eternal Word all things, and therefore also the plant and animal kingdoms, were created. The eternal thoughts of God, which found their embodiment in all creation and thus also in the plant and animal kingdom, only came to be embodied in all creatures through the eternal Word. There is not a flower or a songbird that does not represent something specific from the thoughts of God. . . . The Scriptures do not confine Christ to the realm of grace . . . but place all creation, both the visible and the invisible, here on this earth and below it in direct dependence on Christ. . . . Nothing is thus excluded from the Son. Whatever kingdom of nature, whatever star or comet you wish to take, . . . it is all with the Christ, not in an oblique, but in a direct connection, and there is no power at work in Nature, and there is no law which governs the operation of this power, but it has already proceeded from that eternal Word. It is therefore preposterous to say that although the Christ is in spiritual things, the physical sciences are outside of Him and have no point of contact with Him. In a certain sense it must rather be said that every deeper penetration of knowledge into the nature of Nature glorifies the majesty of the eternal Word.[2]

For Kuyper, the reason for the Christian university is Christ himself. He is the Creator of the universe. Everything was made by him

---

[2] Abraham Kuyper, *Pro Rege*, vol. 1 (Kampen, Holland: J. H. Kok, 1911), 181–82, http://archive.org/details/pro-rege-kuyper-english-vol.-1-pdt.

and for him; *every act of creation was also an act of revelation* intended to show some aspect of the mind of Christ. Whatever facet of creation we study reveals something of the divine mind; we have fully understood nothing until we have seen it in this light. The same line of thought is found in Francis Schaeffer's L'Abri ministry, which sought to challenge the prevailing trends of modern, secular education in the mid-twentieth century:

> [The] life-affirming truth of Christianity speaks to *all* of human life and thought. This means our lives are not divided between "sacred" and "secular" activities, and that Christian *faith integrates all of human life*, including our minds, our hearts, our work, our play, and our relationships. This also means that art, history, philosophy, economics, psychology, education, politics, science, contemporary society, and all other realms of thought can be examined from a biblical viewpoint.[3]

In a modern and secular university, reading the world as an act of divine revelation is not practiced; in fact, it is often directly forbidden. Only naturalistic or humanistic explanations are allowed. Whatever the merits of a secular education are, from a Christian standpoint, it will always be incomplete. For Christians, reading the created order in a Christocentric way is necessitated by sound theology. Thus, not only does the task fall to Christians, but it falls to Christians who are studying and teaching in Christian institutions, since such study is not permitted within the confines of secular schools.

The Christian university, then, broadens the scope of learning beyond what is found in secular schools. Arthur Holmes states that "Christian perspectives can generate a worldview large enough to give meaning to all the disciplines and delights of life and to the whole of a

---

[3] "About L'Abri," English L'Abri, accessed July 26, 2023, https://www.englishlabri.org/about. Emphasis added.

liberal education."[4] Furthermore, human learning and rational capabilities are an expression of the image of God and, therefore,

> to educate the whole person, to encourage disciplined learning and the quest for excellence is a sacred trust. The Christian should give himself . . . to thinking, to the exploration of nature and to the transmission of a cultural heritage, as well as to teaching Christian beliefs and values. . . . There is no room here for a dichotomy between what is secular and what is sacred, for everything about people created in God's image belongs to God—that is, it is sacred.[5]

To summarize, the Christian worldview values education as an end, but it also sees it serving higher purposes. Education helps us steward our divine gifts in service of our fellow creatures as well as for the purpose of knowing and glorifying God. All institutes of higher education have a social trust, but Christian higher education also has a divine trust. In short, Christian higher education exists to nurture the life of the mind and form our souls so that we might better serve the good of humanity and the glory of God.

Inadequate Understandings of Christian Education

Thus far we have sketched out a high-level vision of the potential richness of Christian higher education. The obvious next step is to dig more deeply into this understanding and see what riches we discover. But before we do this, it would be good to identify some understandings of Christian education that are pervasive in our culture but ultimately unsatisfactory for one of three reasons: inadequate expectations, inadequate execution, or inadequate theology.

---

[4] Holmes, *The Idea of a Christian College*, 10.
[5] Holmes, 15–16.

Inadequate expectations

Sometimes Christian universities never intend to embrace the vision of a Christian university sketched above. Perhaps this was because founders never really had a robust Christian vision of a university. Perhaps this is because a critical mass of students, parents, and other stakeholders are not demanding the Christian education we have described. Perhaps this is because some people do not really want a Christian university; they want a "Christian enough" university. Their aspirations (and hence their expectations) are much more modest.

Some feel a university is Christian enough if Christians are not disdained and Christian beliefs are not attacked. They are seeking a Christian haven—a Christian safe space. They want the Christian university to be a fortress and refuge against the storm of secularism. At our own university, it is not uncommon for people to talk about a "Christian bubble" as a sort of safe place. Usually this is meant disparagingly—as tantamount to refusing to deal with reality. But I (Rick) have had more than one student say to me that they actually enjoyed and sought out the bubble—and with good reason. Many came from schools where they felt attacked, unwelcome, or just plain persecuted. They were tired and wanted to be in a place where they can relax and be at home. It is not a bad thing that a Christian university can provide a welcoming home for such students, but it should also provide more than that. It should not just be a place of respite, but also a place of renewal, reenergizing, and redeploying. It should build people up and equip them to deal with the challenges of the place and time where God has put us. It should be a place where students find a worthy calling, not just convalescence and comfort.

Other people are not looking for safety but socialization. A Christian university will have done its job if a person finds Christian friends, or more especially, a Christian spouse. Others want an education with a bit of Bible or theology added to it. Christian thought, in this case, does not permeate the education but rather consists of "spiritual insights" tacked onto the education. Still others are just carrying on a family legacy of Christian education or denominational affiliation. In all these cases, the Christian component of higher education is subordinated to other values—whether for jobs, relationships, or personal security. A side effect of this is that the Christian content of the education is streamlined and minimized so as to save tuition expense and move a student more quickly into his or her career. There is little or no value placed on formation and discipleship, on forming a Christian mind that is not conformed to the world, or on providing a foundation for Christian knowledge that truly unites the sacred and secular into a single whole that is subordinated to the lordship of Christ. Such things are not achieved because they are neither expected nor intended.

Inadequate execution

Another way Christian education can miss the mark is by inadequately pursuing a well-conceived goal. Christian schools are facing enrollment declines, political pressure, social pressure, and conflicting expectations from their donors and constituents. Countless demands diffuse and confuse the implementation of even the best visions of Christian higher education. It is easy for an institution to lose its way not because anti-Christian forces have assaulted it or knocked it off track, but rather because internal leadership has not been attentive enough to where they are going. As Christian scholar Harry Poe writes, "Great Christian institutions have never been 'stolen.' They have always been thrown away by Christians who had no particular interest in them."[6]

Poe is right that great Christian institutions have never been stolen against the will of their Christian leaders, though it is less clear

---

[6] Harry Lee Poe, *Christianity in the Academy: Teaching at the Intersection of Faith and Learning* (Grand Rapids: Baker Academic, 2004), 60.

that leaders have been inclined to "throw away" the Christian vision of their university. "Throwing away" smacks of a disregard, or even disdain for the item in question. In certain instances, this has surely happened, but less commonly than Poe implies. What is far more common is a long, slow "mission drift." Institutions usually lose their mission bit by bit—not lock, stock, and barrel. A good window into mission drift is found in Poe's second phrase: "no particular interest." One can read "particular interest" in either of two ways. First, it can mean that a person does not find the issue particularly interesting. He or she does not really care about it or cares more about other things. A second way to understand this phrase is that people have an interest, but their interest never gets down to the particulars. They have no interest in the details.

It is this second sense that is so important to mission drift. Mission ownership consists of countless daily decisions made with Christian particularity. If the Christianness of a university is only present at convocation, graduation, or in student recruiting brochures, then the university is (at best) being only "generally" Christian. We own our mission if and only if we see how it affects the *particular* things that we are doing, and the particularity of our faith is allowed to speak decisively into daily institutional decisions. The surest way for institutions to drift is for our Christianity to become vague. Once Christianity is vague, a Christian vision can easily be reduced to a Christian *heritage*. The faith is no longer seen through the windshield but rather in the rearview mirror. And if Christianity is seen in the rearview mirror, it is no longer guiding the particulars of daily institutional life. Faculty will fail to cultivate a distinctively Christian imagination for their disciplines; deans will hire faculty for their academic abilities rather than their Christian convictions; donors will care more about endowing buildings than about discipling the next generation; and students and their families will care more about getting a high-paying job than being apprenticed to Jesus for a lifetime.

Inadequate theology

One way our Christian theology can be inadequate is by failing to be particular, but it can also prove inadequate by its approach to particularity. It is much easier to be specific when critiquing errors than when cultivating vision. Critique is necessary, and good theology has always been stimulated by the need to respond to errors. But when critiquing becomes the essential mark of a Christian identity, one is failing at the task of Christian higher education. If Kuyper is right that every act of creation is also an act of revelation, our first task in studying the world is to find truth and insight into the mind of God.

We live in an era that is rich in theological critique but poor in theological vision. It is increasingly common in our culture to identify conservative, orthodox theology by what it opposes. A person or a school is conservative because they are anti-LGBTQ, anti-CRT, anti-woke, or simply anti-liberal. We cannot affirm Christ simply by relentlessly denying culture. No amount of rejection constitutes an affirmation. One cannot build a house just by killing all the termites, and Christians must be carpenters, not just exterminators.

Let me change the metaphor slightly. Several years ago, I (Rick) purchased a house with a large backyard with nothing in it. It had spent the past fifty years in disuse apart from rare occasions when it served as a horse pasture. Weed abatement was an almost impossible task. Nature abhors a vacuum, and the weeds were eagerly honoring nature's call to fill the void. I knew the weeds had to go, but I had to decide if my preferred weapon of warfare would be Roundup to kill the weeds or a spade to plant a garden. In either case, weeds were not to be tolerated, but I had to decide if my organizing vision would be of a garden or of dead weeds. In tending the backyard of human culture, Christians face the same problem. Refereeing culture is like killing weeds.

It is of utmost importance to understand that we are not suggesting that we just plant a Christian flower where a secular weed once stood.

The problem with this approach, and any approach that is critique-centered, is that even if we kill a weed and plant a flower in its stead, *the weeds are still determining the shape of the garden*. What is lacking is the hard work of developing a compelling vision of a Christian garden. It is necessary to identify the ways in which an aspect of creation or culture has been distorted by the fall, corrupted by the world, or exploited for the purposes of Satan, but this must lead to a positive vision for that aspect of creation or culture. We must be able to describe what it would look like if it were once again subject to the lordship of Christ and were awaiting his return. What would a human art such as moviemaking or writing poetry look like when submitted to the lordship of Christ? It is not enough to say, "Different than it does today!" If we sweep the movie house clean of demons and add nothing in its place, it is likely to be filled by seven more demons when we are done. The creation will be used—the only question is what vision will drive that use. If "the earth is the Lord's, and the fullness thereof" (Ps 24:1 KJV), his people should have a vision for stewarding that fullness in God-pleasing ways.

Umbrella and Systemic Universities

One final clarification should be made before probing the particulars of a Christian mind relative to higher education. The vision of Christian education we have just described is expansive and demanding; it cannot be assumed that every (or any) Christian university completely fulfills this vision, or that they even intend to fulfill it. Duane Litfin, former president of Wheaton College, came to realize there were two fundamentally different models of operating in Christian universities—what he called the umbrella model and the systemic model.[7] In the umbrella model, Christian universities seek to provide a space with a wide

---

[7] Duane Litfin, *Conceiving the Christian College* (Grand Rapids: Eerdmans, 2004), 14–27.

variety of voices, but where a "critical mass" of voices will represent the sponsoring Christian tradition. Usually, the board of trustees and the highest levels of university administration have preferential representation from the sponsoring denomination. The faculty, staff, and student body will include people who are unhesitatingly secular, others who are searching, and still others of different faith traditions. The only requirement is that since the institution has made room for their distinctive perspective, they likewise make room for the institution to have its distinctive perspective. In contrast to most secular colleges and universities, Christian scholarship is welcome and encouraged under the umbrella model.

Systemic schools, on the other hand, "seek to make Christian thinking systemic throughout the institution, root, branch, and leaf."[8] What is true of the "critical mass" in the umbrella model is true of all in the systemic model. Though systemic schools will engage ideas from every perspective, they do so from an explicitly Christian viewpoint. Faculty are exclusively Christian, and they intentionally draw out the connections between their academic discipline and the historic Christian faith. Students are introduced to competing voices at every turn, though with a view, in the end, of developing them into effective Christian thinkers.

Clearly, both of Litfin's Christian university models are different from secular institutions in that they actively identify themselves as Christian in their marketing, messaging, and community life. Both will encourage Christian scholarship. Whether or not the critical mass of Christian scholarship at an umbrella institution is sufficient for a thriving community of Christian scholarship is an open question that doubtless depends upon the institution. And in a similar way, for systemic institutions, the level of engagement with competing ideas and the integrity with which they are presented will vary widely. The relative merits of the two models will be weighed and measured differently

---

[8] Litfin, 18.

by different people, and in most cases the choice between the systemic and the umbrella model is settled by choices made at the founding of a university. What is most important for our present purposes is to make sure that boards, faculty, parents, and students all understand the sort of Christian university they are choosing to attend or at which they are serving. The focus of this book is systemic Christian institutions, but what is said will generally apply to the "critical mass" of Christians at umbrella institutions equally well.

The Particulars of the Christian Mind

The remainder of this chapter will attempt some of the particulars that are distinctive to the Christian mind that were sketched in broad strokes at the outset of the chapter. A helpful way to frame this discussion is by way of Abraham Kuyper's inaugural address to the Free University in Amsterdam, in which he stated that "no single piece of our mental world is to be hermetically sealed off from the rest, and there is not a square inch in the whole domain of our human existence over which Christ, who is Sovereign over all, does not cry: 'Mine!'"[9] This is a vivid way to express the lordship of Christ over creation, but how does this actually work out in the life of a Christian university?

View of the cosmos

The Christian faith offers a very distinctive view of the cosmos. We believe in creation ex nihilo—that God made the world out of no preexisting matter and was therefore unconstrained in what he created. This stands in opposition to creation narratives that begin with preexisting matter, as well as those that understand the universe as

---

[9] James Bratt, ed., *Abraham Kuyper: A Centennial Reader* (Grand Rapids: Eerdmans, 1998), 488.

somehow creating itself. Furthermore, since creation is an act of a good God, the created order itself is both real and good; it is neither an illusion as certain Eastern religions understand it to be, nor is it evil as Gnostics understand it to be.

Creation ex nihilo also means that creation is an unconstrained outpouring of the mind of God—it is an act of revelation. The significance of this was brought home to me (Rick) in a conversation I had with one of our Cinema and Media Arts professors. We were participating in a faculty group that was reflecting on the spiritual significance of various cultural artifacts. In this case, the cultural artifact was an excerpt of a television show in which the main character was sitting behind an office desk engaged in a conversation. In our discussion afterward, my colleague made some observations about the set and then pointed out the particular significance of the colors in the picture behind the lead character. She claimed it added an ironic twist to the dialog. I wondered aloud if there was that much to be read out of a background picture on the set. She asked, "Have you ever spent any time on the set of a television show?" When I said that I had not, she said, "I spent fifteen years working on sets. When you first walk into the studio, there is absolutely nothing there. It is an empty room with all the walls painted black. Everything you see on the show was put there by the director for a reason." I immediately realized she was right. I also realized that filling an empty studio is an excellent metaphor for creation ex nihilo. The world was without form and void, and whatever we see within in it now was put there by God's intentional creative activity. Diana Butler describes Calvin's use of similar images when he calls the world a "glorious theater" of God's works. Men and women are placed there as spectators. The universe itself was founded as a spectacle of God's glory.[10]

---

[10] Diana Butler, "God's Visible Glory: The Beauty of Nature in the Thought of John Calvin and Jonathan Edwards," *Westminster Theological Journal* 52, no. 1 (1990): 17.

The cosmos, then, is not simply atoms moving in a void. It is a spectacle awaiting our careful observation and inviting our worship and praise. As we walk out the door in the morning, we walk into a sort of divine movie set in which everything that is present to our senses has been put there by our divine director. The same is true when we walk into the laboratory or library of a university. It is meant to convey to us a message and enrich our understanding of the grand narrative in which God has placed us. The Christian university serves a special role in opening our eyes to all such wonders.

View of truth

Christians affirm the unity of truth. As Augustine put it, "Every good and true Christian should understand that wherever he may find truth, it is his Lord's."[11] On the one hand, this means that truth can be found in the mouths of pagans as well as Christians. So Augustine argued that the alphabet should not be rejected because it was a pagan invention, nor should we refuse justice and virtue simply because pagans build temples to them. Regardless of who made the discovery, if it is true, then it is God's truth. The unity of truth also means that truth is found not only in studying Scripture but in studying the entirety of the created order. The *world* is made by the same God who gave us the *Word*. They both alike bear the stamp of his nature; both can be mined for truth. And, finally, these riches can be mined by pagan and Christian alike. More will be said of this later in our discussion of general and special revelation.

A further development of the unity of truth in Christian theology is that since all truth comes from God, it is meant to hang together. In fact, truths are not understood properly until and unless they are

---

[11] Augustine, *On Christian Doctrine*, trans. J. F. Shaw (Oxford: Benediction Classics, 2010), 2:28.

understood in light of their relationship to all other truth. Therefore, it is important that truth not be isolated from other truths—not only other truths within a specific field of study but all truth. Individual truths are like individual objects in a painting. They are identifiable and describable, but their real significance is the way they stand in relation to everything else in the picture. A university, then, should concern itself with all knowledge viewed as a whole, and students should be broadly educated. Truth that is excluded from the university not only is neglected, but also fails to bring its own influence to bear on all the other truth around it. John Henry Newman puts it this way:

> The various branches of knowledge, which are the matter of teaching in a University, so hang together, that none can be neglected without prejudice to the perfection of the rest, and if Theology be a branch of knowledge . . . to withdraw Theology from the public schools is to impair the completeness and to invalidate the trustworthiness of all that is actually taught in them. . . . In a word, Religious Truth is not only a portion, but a condition of general knowledge. To blot it out is nothing short, if I may so speak, of unravelling the web of University Teaching.[12]

This argument cuts in both directions. Not only is neglecting theology detrimental to all other truths; neglecting other truth diminishes our theology and dilutes and constrains our knowledge of God.

View of knowledge and revelation

The Christian mind sees all human knowledge to be the result of an act of divine revelation. Once again, this is a striking contrast to the

---

[12] John Henry Newman, *The Idea of a University* (New Haven, CT: Yale University Press, 1996), 57.

assumptions about knowledge in a secular context. In the materialistic view of the world common to secular thought, the world is like raw ore waiting to be mined and refined for crystals of truth and knowledge. These crystals then find their place in descriptive theories or are exploited for human purposes. The ore itself does not "mean" anything. Rather, the meaning is imputed by the human mind; the purposes are always human purposes. The ore itself is mere silent stuff; no preexisting meaning or purpose is waiting to be read off its surface.

What is missing in this description is any notion of revelation. Christians adopt, or should adopt, a very different posture toward the created order. For us, it is not "raw" material at all; it is *revelatory* material. Creation was meant to speak to us. It is commonly called general revelation because its voice is *generally* available to all people at all times as they encounter any particular facet of creation. God also reveals himself to people at special places and times, and this we call special revelation. These two sources of revelation are sometimes called the book of nature and the book of Scripture. When we read these books as revelation, we are not treating them as passive objects upon which our imagination can play. Instead, we approach them as a message meant to be read and understood and which contains things God wants us to know about himself and his plans and purposes for the cosmos.

Johannes Kepler, the renowned astronomer, is a great example of this approach. He viewed not only the stars as part of general revelation, but also physics, astronomy, and geometry itself. He believed all these things were grounded in God's nature and that they revealed the pattern by which God created the world and which he passed on to human beings as part of the image of God. Likewise, the laws derived from geometrical and mathematical analysis are things that God intended human beings to discover, because they were intended as acts of revelation. As Kepler writes to the Bavarian chancellor, "Those laws [of nature] are within the grasp of the human mind; God wanted us to recognize them by creating us after his own image so that we could share in his own thoughts."[13]

This revelatory mindset permeates Kepler's book and letters. It was the guiding light for all his inquiries and led to frequent outbursts of praise and gratitude toward God. He wrote to a friend, "I wanted to become a theologian. For a long time I was restless. Now, however, behold how through my effort God is being celebrated in astronomy."[14] His astronomical studies pointed toward a theological end. The result of his efforts was that other people were celebrating the God of the heavens. Kepler sums up his views best in his own words when he writes, "The chief aim of all investigations of the external world should be to discover the rational order and harmony which has been imposed on it by God and which He revealed to us in the language of mathematics."[15]

Kepler is not a unique case. Similar thinking is found in many other Christian scientists over the past four centuries, including other luminaries such as Boyle, Faraday, and Maxwell. But Kepler is helpful because he is so explicit in his theological reflections, especially regarding revelation, the divine nature of creation, and God's image manifested in human reason and its products. Relative to the need for the Christian university, Kepler is also a perfect example of the intellectual power of the revelatory stance, motivating careful research but also inspiring divine praise. We are not arguing that adopting a revelatory stance toward creation made Kepler a better scientist, though it very well may have. Our argument is that adopting a revelatory stance made him a better Christian. Training young Christian scientists to think of

---

[13] Johannes Kepler, "Letter to the Bavarian Chancellor Herwart von Hohenburg," April 1599, collected in Carola Baumgardt and Jamie Callan, *Johannes Kepler Life and Letters* (New York: Philosophical Library, 1953), 50.

[14] Johannes Kepler, "Letter to Michael Maestlin," October 3, 1595, in *Gesammelte Werke*, vol. 13 (Munich: C. H. Beck, 1937), 40.

[15] Morris Kline, *Mathematical Thought from Ancient to Modern Times*, vol. 1 (New York: Oxford University Press, 1972), 231.

the world as Kepler did will also make them better Christians. And it is the job of the Christian university to make better Christians.

View of human flourishing

One way or another, higher education always connects to human flourishing, but what it means to flourish depends in part on what it means to be human. Some see human flourishing as a project of self-discovery and self-expression, while others see human flourishing as something that must be grounded in a fixed human nature. The latter case assumes that human beings have certain universal features that grant all people dignity prior to and independent of the desires, personal abilities, or deeply felt passions any particular person might possess. Moreover, the fixed features of human nature include objective needs and desires and capacities—things that all human beings are made to want or need or do. Any given set of personal desires may or may not correspond with the demands of objective human nature. In fact, human flourishing is largely a project of conforming our felt desires to the reality of human nature.

Christian thought accepts this starting point and builds on it. In the Old Testament, the notion of "shalom" reflects this emphasis on flourishing. It means living as we were created to be. It has the basic meaning of "wholeness," though it is at times translated as "peace." For example, Prov 3:1–2 (NIV) puts it this way:

> My son, do not forget my teaching, but keep my commands in your heart, for they will prolong your life many years and bring you peace [shalom] and prosperity.

Here, the notion of shalom is put in parallel to prosperity, and the idea of flourishing fits well in this context. Similarly, in Ps 29:11 (NIV),

> The LORD gives strength to his people;
> the LORD blesses his people with peace [shalom].

Here, God's blessing is connected with the shalom he provides for his people, and again the notion of flourishing fits the context well. The prophets reflect this concept as well. In Jer 29:7 (NIV), God mandates Israel in exile to "seek the peace [shalom] and prosperity of the city to which I have carried you into exile. Pray to the LORD for it, because if it prospers, you too will prosper." Again, shalom parallels prosperity, reinforcing the idea that shalom is broader than simply "peace" but also can refer to the flourishing of communities.

This parallels the Platonic view of "justice" in the individual's soul (as opposed to social justice). Plato compared the human person to the city (the individual writ large), which functions harmoniously and flourishes when each member of the city fulfills his or her proper function. Plato then applies this to the individual person, which is understood as all the parts of a person working together as a harmonious whole, with each part fulfilling its proper function.[16]

For Christians, the creation narrative identifies the distinctive feature of human nature as being the "image of God." As theologian Louis Berkhof notes: "According to Scripture the essence of man consists in this, that he is the image of God. As such he is distinguished from all other creatures and stands supreme as the head and crown of the entire creation."[17] That is, human beings have an exalted status that none of the rest of God's creation can claim.[18] In the New Testament, the image of God is fulfilled in Christ himself, who in the incarnation becomes the quintessential Image of God. Paul describes him in Col 1:15 as the Image of the invisible God. Hebrews 1:3 describes him

---

[16] Plato, *The Republic*, Book II, sections 368e-373d, particularly 368e-369a, trans. G. M. A. Grube (Indianapolis: Hackett Publishing, 1974), 39–43.

[17] Louis Berkhof, *Systematic Theology* (Grand Rapids: Eerdmans, 1996), 205.

[18] For further discussion of the meaning of the image of God, see John F. Kilner, *Dignity and Destiny: Humanity in the Image of God* (Grand Rapids: Eerdmans, 2015); and Carmen Joy Imes, *Being God's Image: Why Creation Still Matters* (Downers Grove: IVP Academic, 2023).

as the radiance of God's glory and states that he is the exact imprint of his nature. In 1 Cor 15:49, Paul describes Christians as being destined to be transformed into his image, so that just as we are the image of the man of dust, we will also be the image of the man of heaven. If Christ is the quintessential Image of God, and "being God's image" is what it means to be human, then Christ is also the quintessential human. If we want to understand human nature done right, we need look no further than the incarnate Christ. Therefore, all of the "in Christ" language in the New Testament that describes discipleship and sanctification could easily be viewed as a call to become fully human—to live the kind of life Christ lived. The New Testament offers a Christ-centered vision of human flourishing.

For a Christian university to take up the task of "making students fully human," is really just taking up the task of making Christ-followers. When we are formed into his image, we become more truly and more fully human. Obviously, one could neither expect nor demand that this sort of project be done by a secular institution. Even at secular schools that share a commitment to human flourishing, the vision of human flourishing will be different, or at the very least incomplete, in the mind of Christians. This also puts a burden on the Christian university to develop an intentional plan for forming their students into Christlikeness. This plan must be expressed in tangible practices that make sense within the context of higher education. It is dangerous to leave something as important as Christlike formation to practices that are not visible, structured, rewarded, and refined.

Pursuing a Christian vision of human flourishing also means that professors at a Christian school will have a different role relative to their students than their colleagues at a secular institution. They will not only be instructors; they will also be disciplers. Their roles will include mentoring and advising within their disciplines, but they will also serve as models of what it means to be imitators of Christ, apprenticed to him, and devoted to his service. They might be viewed as master apprentices who help younger apprentices live according to the way of Christ. This is a daunting and demanding task for which some professors may feel inadequate. But however inadequate a faculty member may feel, Wendell Berry is right to say that

> there is no one to teach young people but older people, and so the older people must do it. That they do not know enough to do it, that they have never been smart enough or experienced enough or good enough to do it, does not matter. They must do it because there is no one else to do it. This is simply the elemental trial—some would say the elemental tragedy— of human life: the necessity to proceed on the basis merely of the knowledge that is available, the necessity to postpone until too late the question of the sufficiency and the truth of that knowledge.
>
> There is, then, an inescapable component of trial and error in human education; some things that are taught will be wrong because fallible humans are the teachers. But the reason for education, its constant effort and discipline, is surely to reduce the young person's dependence on trial and error as far as possible.[19]

The Christian exemplar of human flourishing is Christ himself— of course we will feel inadequate. However, that cannot dissuade us from performing the task of modeling, guiding, and instructing the students God entrusts to us to the best of our abilities. And it should be noted that making a significant impact on a student is not necessarily as daunting as we make it sound. You do not have to be excellent in doing it; you just need to be interested in doing it. I heard someone tell the story of an economics major who decided to become a math major. He said that he liked economics and did well in his first courses, but after

---

[19] Wendell Berry and Jacques Maritain, *The Loss of the University* (Washington, DC: The Trinity Forum, 2022), 21.

three courses in that department, he never had a professor who offered one word of encouragement, or even criticism. He realized he could not learn like that. He ended up becoming a math major because he met a math professor who really showed some interest in him. That was all it took.

View of calling and vocation

One final uniqueness of the Christian university demands our attention: the Christian view of calling. Contemporary notions of calling tend to center on self-discovery and personal satisfaction. One seeks a calling, usually one that is in part defined by giving expression to one's "true self." Upon finding such a calling, one expects to find true happiness and fulfillment. One can easily see this expectation in the title of the book *Find Your Calling, Love Your Life: Paths to Your Truest Self in Life and Work*. The book states that the "value of our calling is that it requires us to express the most fundamental truths of who we are. Our true life's work returns us to ourselves. Self-recognition and self-acceptance may be our calling's first gifts to ourselves. And the world."[20] Finding a calling, in this understanding, is very much an inward project of identifying one's passions and gifts, and finding a vocational means of expressing them with the ultimate purpose of living a happy and meaningful life. Books like this assume that if you discover something about which you are passionate and which fulfills your vision of your true and authentic self, then you will be able to make a good living. It is summarized by the popular maxim, "Do what you love and the money will follow."[21] However, there is no necessary

---

[20] Martha Finney and Deborah Dasch, *Find Your Calling, Love Your Life: Paths to Your Truest Self in Life and Work* (New York: Simon & Schuster, 1998), 21.

[21] See for example, Marsha Sinetar, *Do What You Love and the Money Will Follow: Discovering Your Right Livelihood* (New York: Dell, 1989). For critique of

connection between doing what you love and earning a living doing it. A person's passion may or may not be in market demand. For example, the world is full of artists who are doing what they love, and who also have side jobs they may not love but that pays their bills. We no longer live in the ancient and medieval world where artists (and intellectuals) routinely had patrons who supported them generously. The above maxim needs to be amended to say the following—"Do what you love and the money will follow, if what you love is something that enough people will pay you for."

In biblical times, the modern, largely secular notion of calling was likely not something individuals thought much about. As a general rule, people followed in the occupational path of their families. The idea of vocational choice (and socio-economic mobility) was something for which ancient men and women had few, if any, opportunities. In fact, in our view, if you transplanted the average person in the first century AD into the typical college or university, Christian or otherwise, and showed them the school's career center, they would likely be mystified at what they were seeing. The trend today toward equating calling/vocation with career is foreign to Scripture. Similarly, seeing calling almost entirely wrapped up with personal satisfaction and passion is, at best, an incomplete view of calling. What you were called to in the New Testament was more a station in life rather than, strictly speaking, an occupation (1 Cor 7:17–20). We are using the terms *calling* and *vocations* interchangeably and would define a vocation as *an arena of service to which God has called a person*. One normally has multiple vocations, to which God has called him or her, with numerous obligations to be fulfilled *all at the same time*. That is, they are simultaneous, not sequential. For example, I (Scott) have vocations as a husband, father, professor,

---

Sinetar, see Jay W. Richards, *The Human Advantage: The Future of Work in an Age of Smart Machines* (New York: Forum Books, 2018).

neighbor, church member, among others, with obligations in each arena to be fulfilled simultaneously.

It is easy to see why an individualized notion of calling is attractive to a world caught up in individualism and personal happiness, but it is strongly at odds with a Christian understanding of calling. Particularly during and immediately after the Reformation, Christian conceptions of calling were the subject of intensive theological reflection. They began by making a fundamental distinction between general calling—to salvation and sanctification—and specific callings, which relate to our work and service. William Perkins, an influential English Puritan theologian, wrote extensively on the nature of our specific callings. He begins with a definition of specific calling: "A vocation or *calling is a certain kind of life, ordained and imposed on man by God for the common good.*"[22] Notice that for Perkins, the origin and purpose of a calling are both external to oneself. Calling *originates* in God, and its *purpose* is the common good. This is almost exactly opposite of the understanding of calling given above where callings originate from within our own hearts and serve the purpose of our own happiness. What accounts for Perkins's radically different view? The reason is easy to discern.

> The author of every calling is God himself . . . every man is to live as he is called of God. For look as in the camp, the General appoints to every man his place and standing . . . and therein [he is] to live and die. Even so it is in human societies: God is the General appointing to every man his particular calling, . . . in performance whereof he is to live and die. . . . Again, in a

---

[22] William Perkins, *The Workes of That Famous and Worthie Minister of Christ, In the Universitie of Cambridge, M.W. Perkins*, vol. 1 (London: I. Legate, 1605), 903. The modern phrasing, with emphasis added, is from William Perkins, *The Works of William Perkins*, ed. J. Stephen Yuille, Joel R. Beeke, and Derek Thomas, vol. 10 (Grand Rapids: Reformation Heritage Books, 2014).

clock, . . . there be many wheels, . . . some turn this way, some that way, some go slowly, some apace: and they are all ordered by the motion of the watch. Behold here a notable resemblance of God's special providence over mankind, which is the watch of the great world, allotting to every man his motion and calling. . . . Therefore it is true that I say, that God himself is the author and beginning of callings.[23]

Perkins likens God to a general and Christians to soldiers in his army. Clearly, a general must be concerned with winning the battle, not the happiness of an individual soldier. Likewise, the wheels of a clock move in a way that only makes sense when viewed as a whole. In both cases, these ultimate and external purposes are far more significant than the concerns of the individual. And just as the purpose of the call lies external to the person who receives it, likewise the origin of the call is not from within but from without. Callings originate with the general (or the watchmaker) and confront the individual as a command rather than a choice. It is, in Perkins's words, an imposition. One could summarize Perkins's understanding of Christian callings in three essential points:

1. **Callings are not chosen;** they are imposed on people as a matter of logical and theological necessity. Calling, by the meaning of the word, is always from one person to another. Therefore, as a matter of logical necessity, they originate externally to the person who receives the call.
2. **Calling is often unintelligible at an individual level.** A full account of a call is always larger than a single individual. Perkins illustrates this by appeal to the gears in a watch that individually have confused and unintelligible motions. These motions

---

[23] Perkins, 1:903.

only make sense when viewed as part of a shared project—the steady motion of the clock's hands, which tell the time.

3. **Callings serve the good of others.** Callings focus on the good of other people, and they are a way we fulfill the divine command to love our neighbor. They are not primarily a way to please ourselves.

If Perkins is right in his understanding of callings, the Christian university's mission relative to post-graduate employment will have a distinctively different emphasis than that of the prevailing culture. First, one might call into question the very language of "finding a calling." A calling can hardly go missing. Perkins says, "Every person of every degree, state, sex, or condition without exception must have some personal and particular calling to walk in."[24] This is a view of calling students can begin to understand and practice even while they are in school. Students may not have yet identified a career, but they should still have a sense of calling. They are, presumably, called to be students. They are also called to be children to their parents, members of a church, and active participants in their communities. Therefore, they have multiple vocations to which they are called and for which they are responsible, all at the same time. Students need not to go out and seek a calling but to begin living their lives as if their present circumstances constituted a calling. Graduating and entering a career will add another aspect of calling, but it will only be an addition. They are already called.

One misunderstanding of calling/vocation that is more prevalent in Christian colleges and universities is establishing a hierarchy of occupational callings. That is, some callings are deemed more valuable to God and more directly related to God's kingdom than others. For example, pastors and missionaries are commonly seen as having "higher callings" than those who work in business, the professions, or what is

---

[24] Perkins, 1:909.

traditionally called "blue collar" work. Another way to put this is that the alleged higher callings have intrinsic value to God and his kingdom, but the other arenas of service in the marketplace have instrumental value only. Pastors, missionaries, and anyone who gets a paycheck from a church or religious organization is in "full-time ministry," or simply "in ministry." By definition, that leaves the workplace person in either part-time, or no-time, ministry. This often results in a sense that he or she is doing something "less than" for God and his kingdom than those presumed to be in "full-time ministry." To be fair, we see this hierarchy in secular settings as well, with the notion of working for a nonprofit being of more value than being in business.

In our view, this is an incomplete view of calling/vocation that resurrects the sacred-secular dichotomy that was prevalent in the medieval world and that the Reformation sought to do away with. For example, Luther held that there is such a thing as a worldly calling, meaning that one did not have to be cloistered in a monastery to be of service to God. As a result, all believers are in full-time ministry (or service, as the more common translation of *diakonia*), and they enter full-time service at the time they come to faith in Christ. And no one leaves full-time service—they simply change arenas of service when they change jobs. In our view, it is important to recognize that there is no hierarchy of callings, no calling that is higher than another, and no distinction between the sacred and secular. It may mean that certain arenas of service are a better fit for a specific person, given his or her gifts and skills. But that is not to say that they are *objectively* better or of greater service to God.

It is critically important to realize that God ordained work *prior* to the general entrance of sin in Genesis 3 (it was ordained in Gen 1:27 and repeated in 2:15), thus giving all legitimate work intrinsic value to God and to his service. This is reaffirmed in Col 3:23–24 (NIV): "Whatever you do, work at it with all your heart, as working for the Lord, not for human masters, since you know that you will receive an inheritance from the Lord as a reward. It is the Lord Christ you are serving." This was written to household servants (see v. 22) who did arguably the most mind-numbing, tedious work in the ancient world. Yet their work was, according to Paul, service to Christ. Lest we think that one's service to Christ in the workplace involves only "spiritual matters" such as praying for coworkers, sharing the gospel with them, and having compassion for them in times of need (all good and necessary activities), all those things are things believers are doing *when they are not doing their job*. Paul's emphasis is that *the very work itself* is part of their service to Christ, which is why it is to be done with excellence.

In summary, Christian thinking should be profoundly less self-centered than our prevailing culture, have an eye to the common good, and value all vocations equally as service of God. Personal gifts and desires are not irrelevant to discerning a calling. After all, Christians view our souls as crafted by God in our mother's womb. If God appoints us a particular calling, we would rightly expect it to make sense of the particular qualities that he built into us. These qualities, however, do not have the final say. We serve bigger purposes, kingdom purposes, which may require us to do things that we would never do if all that mattered were our personal preferences. A Christian university should also intentionally remind students that a calling is a call to service, not self-fulfillment or personal advancement. A Christian university should be intentional about how callings are presented not only in classrooms but also in career counseling, faculty mentoring, chapel messages, and in other cocurricular activities.

Conclusion

The theologian and historian Robert Benne describes Christian thought as offering a comprehensive account that encompasses all of life. This account persists through time, claims to be the vehicle of ultimate truth, and definitively addresses all the essential questions of life: meaning, purpose, and conduct. Ultimately, he argues, if another account of life surpasses the Christian story in the lives of believers, they no longer legitimately claim to be Christians.[25] For Christian institutions of higher education, the Christian story must be *the* story, not simply one among many. This does not limit the scope of Christian education—it simply defines the perspective. It will cultivate the life of the mind for the sake of human flourishing, but it will have a particular view of what it means for humans to flourish.

Christian education seeks to cultivate the life of the mind for the good of humanity and the glory of God. Christian concern for the glory of God means we are intentional about thinking God's own thoughts after him. We read not only Scripture but the created order in a revelatory fashion. Once this has been done well, Christians participate in human culture-building efforts, but those efforts will be meant to value and shape the world in God-pleasing ways. The scope of the Christian vision of reality makes sense of the need for fully Christian institutions of higher education.

Questions

1. What would it mean for a university to be "Christian enough"? What aspects are essential if an institution of higher education is to be considered Christian?

2. One major point this chapter makes is that we need to be concerned about the "particularity" of our Christian mission. It warns that being "vaguely" Christian is likely to result in mission drift. Think about your own institution. Is its Christian faith expressed in particular and specific structures, commitments, hiring practices, and curriculum design? Identify these particularities and reflect on

---

[25] Robert Benne, *Quality with Soul: How Six Premier Colleges and Universities Keep Faith with Their Religious Traditions* (Grand Rapids: Eerdmans, 2001), 6–7.

how effective they are and how they might be clarified or strengthened. If the Christian faith seems to be vaguely expressed, reflect on
whether this is by design or by neglect.

3. A set of particulars about the Christian mind is given in this chapter
    (a particular way of viewing the cosmos, truth, knowledge, human
    flourishing, and calling). Reflect on how these issues are understood
    in your own educational context. What are you doing particularly
    well at, and what could be improved?

CHAPTER 3

WHAT IS *OUR* CHRISTIAN UNIVERSITY?

The first question we should ask is not: What should we cut, in order to be financially viable? Our first question should be: What must we keep—at all costs—in order to be faithful to what God has called us to be and do? The mission question for us should be first—not merely one criterion among others.

N ot every Christian university is the same. Some differences are plain to see, such as a church affiliation in the name of a school. Some differences reside in the scope of the institution: some are Bible colleges, some are liberal arts colleges, and still others are universities. Some began as distinctively Christian schools but have drifted from their original mission in such a way that there is little difference today between them and a secular university. Some are Christian by institutional affiliation and structure; others seek to embed their Christian faith throughout all curricula. Some reflect a more progressive political and theological stance, while others are more conservative on both counts. Some require a statement of Christian faith from students prior to admission, while others admit students regardless of where their faith journey has taken them, thus making for somewhat different educational experiences for students. Although Christian universities may share a common vision and their mission statements may sound similar, they have different origins, histories, geographical locations, social contexts, and legacies. Given this diversity, it is imperative that each institution knows itself—that it understands what makes their university distinct from other Christian colleges. They should also communicate those distinctions clearly to stakeholders and shareholders, especially students, faculty, and donors.

Understanding and expressing the core identity of an educational institution is not as simple as writing a mission statement. Universities are living communities of people. They cannot be reduced to a pithy statement or a list of beliefs or a timeline of events. What is needed is an understanding of what animates the organization—what might be called the *sacred core*. The sacred core is something that grows from the seeds planted by the founders and is tended by all those who have served the organization in the ensuing years. It includes things like mission, values, and goals, but it also includes historical events, defining moments, and a host of intangibles things, both small and large, that have served to animate, inspire, and direct ongoing community life. A good example of this concept can also be found in the "sacred bundle"— an important part of tribal identity for many Indian tribes in the North American plains.[1] The sacred bundle preserved cultural identity by literally collecting parts of their tribal history in a bag or animal hide. It

---

[1] John Bare, "Evaluation and the Sacred Bundle," Harvard Family Research Project, Summer 2005, https://archive.globalfrp.org/evaluation/the-evaluation-exchange/issue-archive/evaluation-methodology/evaluation-and-the-sacred-bundle; Joshua J. Mark, "Making the Sacred Bundle," World History Encyclopedia, October 4, 2023, https://www.worldhistory.org/article/2290/making-the-sacred-bundle/; Melissa Addey, "The Sacred Bundle: A Magical Way to Express Your Core Business Values," Innovation and Enterprise Blog,

might contain a rock, feather, or other small token that represented an important person or event in tribal history. In tribal gatherings, items from the sacred bundle would be drawn out, and their stories would be told to all who were present. Over time, everyone in the tribe came to know and find his or her identity in these shared stories.

In a modern setting, we do not gather around a fire and tell stories, but there are other practices that reinforce organizational identity. Key events and decisions often accumulate in a rather ad hoc manner over the course of years, and this actually makes the "sacred bundle" a helpful metaphor. For example, "Jesus Saves" is a common phrase used by Christians, but it has a special meaning for us at Biola. It was made into a neon sign that was put atop our first major building in the heart of downtown Los Angeles and adorned the skyline there for decades. Pictures of the sign appear frequently in Biola literature and sometimes in historical photographs of the city of Los Angeles. The phrase itself commonly appears in papers and documents as a reminder of one of the most deeply held beliefs of our founders.

Another item in our sacred bundle is the Red Book. Since the early days of our founding, the trustees have signed the "Worker's Register and Articles of Faith" (known as the "Red Book") every year. The signing of the Red Book is now a formal public event as an outward expression of Biola's commitment to its core mission and values. A more recent slogan that could be considered part of our sacred bundle is the phrase, "Think biblically about everything." It was used in some marketing campaigns and was on the marquee at the front gate of our campus in conjunction with a rolling list of academic disciplines (Think biblically about . . . business, psychology, education, etc.). This phrase has stuck with us and is commonly used as shorthand for our commitment to integrating faith and learning.

April 27, 2016, https://blogs.bl.uk/business/2016/04/the-sacred-bundle-a-magical -way-to-express-your-core-business-values.html.

We also have a forty-foot-high mural of Jesus holding out a Bible that was painted by a well-known muralist in Los Angeles. The mural has been the source of controversy since some feel he looks too white (ethnically). Some have suggested it be painted over, but others have responded by saying that the day the Jesus mural is painted over is the day that they will resign from their job. This is a good illustration that the sacred bundle is not always made of the same items for everyone, or at the very least, people will respond to various items differently. Nonetheless, an item could only make it into the sacred bundle if it evokes strong feelings. These items are not great achievements that we are particularly proud of; they are just artifacts of Biola's history that have taken on special meaning within our community. They are listed here in the hope they will recall analogous items, slogans, or practices that contribute to the sacred bundle of other Christian colleges or universities that our readers identify with. The same can be said of all the illustrations that will be given throughout this chapter.

In the discussion that follows, we will generally use the language of "sacred core"—though core ideology, or sacred bundles might work equally well. The point of all these concepts is to make visible key aspects of the community DNA—things that animate our college or university and that all members of the community should know, believe, value, celebrate, and aspire toward. We will discuss the sacred core by examining its roots in the founders, and then consider how it is maintained and operationalized in the ongoing life of the university.

Roots of a Sacred Core

The language of sacred core naturally points back to our institutional roots as they are seen in the lives of the institution's founders. It invites questions like, "What did those who founded our institution hold dear?" and, "What prompted our founders to make the enormous sacrifices of time, treasure, and energy necessary to found a university?" Thinking about founders also invites us to think about their mission. What issues confronted them, and how did those issues crystalize into a strategic mission that could best be addressed by creating an institution of higher education? And why did they innovate and create a new institution rather than jumping on some already existing bandwagon?

Founders and their mission

The point of looking at institutional founding is not anchoring an institution in the past. A better way of thinking about it is as a way of determining institutional trajectory. The founders determined what might be called the *intended* sacred core. But all of those who came after them, taken together, have determined the *functional* sacred core. The functional sacred core is what has remained, what has continued to guide decisions again and again through the years. Every generation of leaders inherits *both* sacred cores—the intended and the functional—and to that inheritance they contribute their own decisions, their own resources, and their own passion. In short, they make their own revisions and contributions to the functional core. They never really get to start over—there are no clean slates in institutional life. Nor should there be. Institutions are created for the exact reason of preserving a vision and mission and passing it on to the next generation. The founders are like parents—they gift us their DNA. And just like the genetic DNA we inherit from our parents, though it is in one sense fixed, it is not static. The expression of our DNA is influenced in profound ways by environmental factors—both at the time of founding and also through all succeeding generations. Attending to the interplay of the joint factors of organizational DNA and cultural influences is the constant and demanding job of all institutional leaders.

As an example of how the DNA of founders combines with other cultural and historical factors to determine what "genes" are actually expressed, consider these two mission statements drawn from their respective college websites:

The mission of Occidental College is to provide a gifted and diverse group of students with a total educational experience of the highest quality—one that prepares them for leadership in an increasingly complex, interdependent, and pluralistic world.

The mission of Biola University is biblically centered education, scholarship and service—equipping men and women in mind and character to impact the world for the Lord Jesus Christ.

The obvious difference between these two mission statements is the secular language of the first and the sacred language of the second. Anyone who knows the two schools would find this difference unsurprising. Though Occidental and Biola are universities located in close proximity to each other, and though they were founded within a few years of one another, they are clearly worlds apart in terms of their stated mission and ethos. One might anticipate that the differences between the two schools could be found in differences between their two founders. This would be a mistaken assumption.

Occidental and Biola make a perfect example of the combination of factors that go into "institutional gene expression." Lyman Stewart, a California oilman, was deeply invested in the founding of both institutions, and in that sense Occidental and Biola have similar initial DNA. In both cases, he played a pivotal role in terms of financial resources and also in actively recruiting key leaders in the early years of the respective colleges' founding. Today, however, if you were to search Biola's website, you would find a multitude of references to Lyman Stewart. The same search of Occidental's website would yield a single reference to Stewart as one of two trustees who together personally guaranteed an extremely generous salary required to woo the second president of the institution, Dr. John Willis Baer, who came with a vision for making Occidental the "Princeton of the West." Unfortunately, that vision contributed to an unexpected theological turn and ultimately to abandoning historic Christian orthodoxy. In short, Occidental aligned with the modernist side of what has been called the modernist/fundamentalist controversy. This was, in Stewart's estimation, the wrong side of one of the most important issues of the day. And that experience gave him a sense of mission—to launch a school that would be explicitly tied to Christian orthodoxy from its earliest days and built to preserve that tie to orthodoxy as long as the Lord should tarry.

Lyman Stewart's sense of mission was not his uniquely. It is one variation of a theme that emerges from the simmering fundamentalist/modernist controversies that raged in the late nineteenth and early twentieth centuries. The result was an increasing marginalizing and cultural discrediting of the fundamentalists. This led many conservative Christian leaders to abandon mainline Christian schools and develop parallel cultural institutions that would be faithful to Christian orthodoxy. Notable among these are people such as D. L. Moody (Moody Bible Institute), A. B. Simpson (Nyack College), and A. J. Gordon (Gordon College and Gordon-Conwell Theological Seminary), in addition to Lyman Stewart (Biola University).[2] These schools often sprang up for the purpose of educating pastors and missionaries, but it was not uncommon for them to expand their offerings, at first developing medical or nursing schools to train medical missionaries, and ultimately developing into liberal arts colleges and universities.

So Lyman Stewart was one of many college founders who were concerned with doctrinal fidelity. In the case of Biola's founding documents, he wove this into our DNA by assuring that the doctrinal statement could not be changed, even by the Board of Trustees, without

---

[2] For this historical sketch, we are indebted to Barry H. Corey, "Biola's Faithful Crossing Initiative: A Missional Retrospective and Missional Blueprint," (unpublished paper, March 1, 2021). This was one of several periodic looks backward to Biola's founding and founders' intentions that clarified the mission of the university going forward.

triggering a clause that would require returning funds to the original donors. As one might imagine, this was an effective mechanism that continues to shape Biola to this day. Furthermore, the signing of the Red Book mentioned earlier in the chapter was a way of assuring doctrinal commitment among all of Biola's highest level of leadership. Stewart and the other founders of Biola were resolute in their desire to put safeguards in place to ensure long-term doctrinal fidelity in Biola, and the effectiveness of those safeguards is visible today in the mission statements on the college websites.

Founders can be viewed very differently depending on the legacy of the institution. In some schools, the founders are revered visionaries, and each new generation is held accountable for maintaining the founders' vision and intentions for the school. In other cases, the founders are largely ignored or considered a source of mild to moderate embarrassment to contemporary students and faculty. And in some schools, the founders are viewed as a cautionary tale from which faculty and leadership in the school actively distance themselves. To give a well-known example, many of the Ivy League schools were founded as educational institutions for the training of ministers. That was Harvard's initial goal. As they drifted from that mission, Yale was founded to take up that mantle, and when they likewise drifted, Princeton was founded. In all these cases, the mission was intentionally changed by leaders who wanted to distance themselves from their founders.

In recent years, both Wheaton College and Southern Seminary have wrestled with the legacy of their founders and key leaders, even as they have worked to preserve their mission. In the case of Wheaton, it was founded by abolitionists shortly before the Civil War, but by the 1920s, substantial sentiments of racism were to be found in the comments of the university president. In the case of Southern Seminary and the Southern Baptist denomination, their founding was directly associated with defending slavery as racist sentiments continued to appear in comments of key leaders for many decades.[3] In both cases, the institutions have made substantial efforts to acknowledge the complexity of their founding legacy. As Philip Ryken, president of Wheaton, put it,

> Sometimes you see the glory of God more clearly in his redeeming grace for fallen sinners. We have lots of examples in Scripture of the people of God wrestling with their past and seeking to understand their past, in some cases celebrating, but also lamenting and repenting. There is a complexity about the past that the Scriptures do not back away from but lean into. And that's what we want to do too.[4]

All in all, it is vital that the founding legacy of an institution is understood and valued as an essential part of the organizational DNA. The exact nature of how that is best done varies by the legacy that the founders represent and how that is viewed by current leadership. There are no simple answers to these questions. Founders may be sacred, anti-sacred, or a bit of both.

Maintaining a Sacred Core

What does missional fidelity to an institution and its founders demand in our present moment? Certain culture issues moved the founders to act in a particular way, but cultural issues are constantly changing. Mechanically following the footsteps of the founders, or simply

---

[3] "Report on Slavery and Racism in the History of the Southern Baptist Theological Seminary," December 18, 2018, https://sbts-wordpress-uploads .s3.amazonaws.com/sbts2023/uploads/2023/10/Racism-and-the-Legacy-of -Slavery-Report-v4.pdf.

[4] Daniel Silliman and Kate Shellnutt, "Wheaton College Releases Report on Its History of Racism," *Christianity Today*, September 14, 2023, https://www .christianitytoday.com/news/2023/september/wheaton-college-race-racism -report-task-force.html.

continuing to hold the ground on doctrinal issues that the founders faced, may actually fail to preserve their real legacy. In the early twentieth century, the virgin birth was a central doctrinal issue that played an important role in the fundamentalist/modernist controversy. Today, the virgin birth is still part of historical Christian orthodoxy, but it is not a raging source of controversy. On the other hand, no one in the early twentieth century was thinking about transgenderism, whereas it is almost impossible for Christians not to think about that issue today. Revisiting past doctrinal disputes can actually lead to irrelevance rather than missional fidelity. If one's founders were concerned with preserving the faith once for all delivered to the saints, the best way to honor their legacy will much more likely involve accurately understanding the controversies and temptations of our own day, rather than refighting the battles of our founders' day.

A valuable exercise in maintaining the sacred core of an institution is to ask what the founders' mission would translate into in today's world. Here is a good way to do this. Imagine that your school currently does not exist but that it is financially feasible at present to start a school. What issues are present in the culture that might lead your leaders and donors to found your institution today? How would they respond to these issues, and how would current stakeholders view this response?

An exercise like this will help to clarify the sacred core of your school. As has been noted, this exercise may reveal a distance or tension between your founding sacred core and the functional sacred core that is operating within your school today. If so, this should be acknowledged, probed, clarified, and owned by current leaders. In many cases, however, this exercise will reveal core commitments that you love about your institution and would never give up. In fact, it may be that you would seriously consider closing the doors of the institution rather than give up those commitments. These core commitments are not always listed on the website or written into founding documents, but often must be picked up by osmosis as people live in the university community and absorb the unwritten commitments and commandments. When these are viewed in conjunction with the threats and weaknesses of the institution, as well as the opportunities afforded you by your location and resources, you may get a better sense of what God is specifically calling your particular institution to at this particular time.

Clarifying the sacred core does not solve all controversies, but it should help mark out the playing field for controversies. For example, at many theologically conservative schools, the inerrancy and authority of Scripture is a sacred core issue. One can certainly have a disagreement about what this means for women's roles within the church or about policy decisions in the public square. Members of a faculty may have very substantial disagreements on many issues, but if the authority of Scripture is part of the sacred core, it is "out of bounds" to respond to a scriptural passage that opposes your position simply saying that the Bible is wrong. If inerrancy is part of one's sacred core, one's reasoning must honor, not abandon, the authority of Scripture.

To give another example, let us return to the modernist/fundamentalist controversy mentioned earlier in this chapter. A specific cultural movement at that time was called the "Social Gospel movement." The Social Gospel movement was a central part of the modernist side of this controversy. Leading figures in the Social Gospel movement, like Walter Rauschenbusch, believed that individuals could only leave sinful lifestyles if their social context were changed since their social context was really what led them to a life of sin in the first place. Individual salvation, which was so highly valued by the fundamentalists, was only of secondary importance to issues related to social reform.[5] The fundamentalist side of this controversy saw things very differently. Individual salvation was primary, and in its absence no

---

[5] William R. Hutchison, *The Modernist Impulse in American Protestantism* (Cambridge, MA: Harvard University Press, 1976).

top-down change in social structures could ever sustain real change and advance the kingdom of God.

An interesting question for schools that were founded in part by a reaction against the Social Gospel movement of the early twentieth century is to ask what they should make of the social justice movement of the early twenty-first century. There are many Christian leaders that seem to embrace aspects of the Social Gospel movement when writing about social justice today. There are real and important differences between the Social Gospel movement and the social justice movement, but there are also real similarities. We have heard faculty members at Christian schools say something like, "Social justice just is the gospel." But what then becomes of the gospel of salvation by grace through faith in Jesus Christ? Are the gospel of salvation by grace through faith and the gospel of social justice really the same thing? This was clearly not the view of those who rejected the modernist position in the early 1900s—why then should we see things differently in the early twenty-first century?

On the other hand, I (Rick) was teaching a class that discussed, among other things, the relocation of Japanese citizens to internment camps in World War II. The class took a field trip to the Japanese-American museum in downtown Los Angeles. While we were there, we walked through a whole exhibit about Japanese-American relations in California in the early 1900s. I was shocked to see that election campaign posters for the incumbent senator for California used the slogan, "Keep California White." Like many other politicians of the day, he was rallying support by promising to end "The Yellow Peril"—the threat of Japanese and Chinese immigration. This, combined with a host of other propaganda from the day, got our students thinking about what Biola had done during that era. They set out to look through our archives and the *King's Business* magazine that Biola published for several of its early decades. They discovered that Biola largely ignored these issues. When one of our students was sent to the relocation camps, our monthly magazine simply described him heading out to the camp and asked people to pray that he would be able to effectively share the gospel with fellow internees. Apparently, no one was concerned with whether or not the gospel would condone the internment of American citizens who had done nothing wrong.

What then is the best way to honor the legacy of our founders? Should we preach the gospel of salvation by faith and ignore injustices within our society? Should we equate the gospel of Christ with social justice? Or must we find some ground to stand on between these two extremes? In the discussion in my own class, it was very helpful to have students read some comments by theologian John Stott, who argued against the tendency to make social justice either superior or subordinate to evangelism. Stott felt that making social justice superior to calling people to be reconciled to God through Christ was clearly incompatible with New Testament teaching. But at the same time, he argued against viewing social activism as merely an instrumental good to be used for wooing prospective converts. This, he felt, diminished neighbor love to being the bait on the evangelistic hook as opposed to the fulfillment of one of the two great commandments. Therefore, according to Stott, our social action is not justified by appeal to evangelistic results, "but rather simple, uncomplicated compassion. Love has no need to justify itself."[6]

Sacred core and diversity of thought

Maintaining a theological core is not to prohibit diversity of thought and free expression. Christian commitment to diversity of thought and free expression is grounded in what makes for good education of students. We have no interest in educating students in an echo chamber,

---

[6] John Stott, *Christian Mission in the Modern World*, updated and expanded by Christopher J. H. Wright (Downers Grove: IVP Books, 2015), 30.

nor do we believe that students are so fragile that they need to be protected from ideas that will challenge them and even make them uncomfortable. Such a commitment to diversity of thought and free expression strengthens the educational mission of the school. As we have stated in our own university documents, "Convictions are healthier when they are not cordoned off from—but rather engaged in—rigorous and collegial dialogue with other points of view. Only when students have sincerely considered diverse viewpoints will they as Christ's disciples come to convictions that will weather the test of time and be prepared to engage a complex and diverse world."[7]

This commitment includes not only the substance of ideas with which students engage but also the way this engagement occurs. We should be committed to a style of engagement that is respectful, civil, and represents different views fairly and with kindness. That is not to say that this precludes rigorous challenges when disagreement occurs. We reject the notion that disagreement itself constitutes offense or even hatred, though the way a difference in opinion is expressed may cross the line. This commitment to diversity of thought is not a corresponding commitment to intellectual relativism in which all ideas are equally valid. Within a Christian worldview, Christian wisdom involves discerning truth from error and good from evil, accepting what is true and challenging what is false, with graciousness and civility.

Of course, a commitment to free expression does not accept all expression as valid. Christian schools should not tolerate illegal forms of expression such as "defamation, obscenity, intimidation, threats and incitement to violence . . . harassment, hateful speech, or bullying. . . .

---

[7] We are indebted in this section of the defense of free expression to the "Biola University Statement on Principles of Free Expression and Diversity of Thought." For access to the full statement, see https://www.biola.edu/about/mission/principles-free-expression.

We also reject the notion that disagreement or attempts at persuasion necessarily constitute harassment, hate or bullying."[8]

Boundaries on free expression

Since one of the functions of a university is to maintain a robust freedom of thought, in Christian universities, that occurs within established theological boundaries and in the appropriate venues. Even secular universities recognize that there are boundaries on this and that there is a time and place for this to happen. In fact, we would suggest that in many secular universities, there is a rigid orthodoxy that has taken hold, creating a new absolutism in the form of "cancel culture" and causing widespread skepticism about their commitment to genuine free expression. We think a good argument can be made that there might be more diversity of thought in Christian colleges and universities than in most secular universities. As a rule, we would suggest that the more academic the venue and the more space there is for students to process what is taught under faculty direction, the more latitude there is for freedom of inquiry and diversity of thought. These more academic settings include the classroom (particularly more upper-division classes and major classes), symposia, lectureships, and debates. Less academic settings include chapels, commencement, convocation, donor events, and student recruitment events. In these latter settings, students do not normally have the opportunity to process what they have heard, and the guidance of faculty members is not usually available in these less academic venues.

This assumes that the school has some fundamental theological commitments and that they are a matter of public record, available to anyone who wishes to see them. However, the breadth of any school's

---

[8] "Biola University Statement on Principles of Free Expression and Diversity of Thought."

doctrinal boundaries varies widely, as does the degree to which they are publicly available. Some schools have an extensive theological core to which they are committed, while others have a smaller core and more flexibility on theological matters that they consider outside that core. We would suggest that at a minimum, any Christian college or university be clear about its fundamental doctrinal positions since they significantly contribute to establishing the institutional identity of the school. These must be clear, both internally with those required to hold to them and externally in communications with constituencies such as parents of students and donors.

Operationalizing a Sacred Core

Doctrinal beliefs

One of the most common ways that Christian colleges operationalize their sacred core is by having faculty, staff, and board members, or some subset of these groups, affirm a doctrinal statement or confession of faith. Other schools accomplish a similar purpose by requiring faculty to be members in good standing of a particular denomination. As we have already pointed out, this is not sufficient to ensure mission ownership, but it is a helpful step in that direction. When making such an affirmation, it is usually good to make the affirmation written and also to have it regularly repeated—either annually or with the signing of each contract for faculty. People's views often change, and if doctrinal affirmations are to be taken seriously, they cannot be made once and for all time at the point of hire.

It is also important to clarify exactly what the board intends by having faculty, staff, or board members sign the doctrinal statement. For example, in some discussions we had with faculty members, this question came up, and it was helpful to identify a set of postures a faculty member might have relative to the institution's doctrinal statements.

1. I affirm with equal zeal all of the theological distinctives and articles of faith.

2. I affirm all of the theological distinctives and articles of faith, though I do not have an equal sense of conviction or confidence about all of them. That is to say, in some cases I have no doubts or questions at all, and in some cases I am not fully convinced of my positions but hold them because I know of no other position that seems better to me.

3. I do not personally affirm a certain theological distinctive(s) or article of faith, but I am totally fine with those who do, and I would never teach against it.

4. I disagree with this distinctive and think Biola should change it; however, I consider this a minor issue, and I am happy to major on the majors and let the minors slide.

In our case, it was helpful that the Board of Trustees intends that affirming the Articles of Faith and the Theological Distinctive means either of the first two postures and neither of the second two postures.

Mission planning and budgeting

An important part of mission ownership is how it is translated into planning and budgeting. Earlier in this chapter we mentioned the idea of a "sacred bundle" as another way to conceive of a sacred organizational core. John Bare, a vice president for the Arthur M. Blank Family Foundation, argues that clearly stated institutional values are vital for identifying good outcomes, something that is extremely important to nonprofit organizations trying to meet the demands of donors to document their results. Bare argues that if organizations learn to "measure what you value, and others will value what you measure." He recommends identifying a metaphorical "sacred bundle," complete with stories about the items in the bundle, in order to figure out what the organization values so dearly that it will track it in real time, so that staff can celebrate what is working well and so that they can make adjustments when things get off track.[9] In this way, Bare is operationalizing the sacred core.

We have had a couple of experiences in recent years that bring this to mind. In particular, a prioritization process was implemented to help reduce costs and make for long-term financial viability. The methodology that was adopted was a "best practice" for institutions of higher learning, but it was designed and used largely in secular institutions. Mission-related issues were listed as the ninth of ten factors guiding recommendations. When the prioritization process was implemented and generated a series of recommendations, some seemed completely untenable. A colleague wrote to the university leadership, noting that unlike most all secular universities from which this prioritization procedure had been drawn, our school is first and foremost a mission-driven school. Without our distinctive Christian mission, we really have no reason to exist. Therefore, he said,

> The first question *we* should ask, concerning prioritization, is not: What should we *cut*, in order to be financially viable? Our first question should be: What must we *keep*—at all costs—in order to be faithful to what God has called us to be and do? The mission question for us should be *first*—not merely one criterion among others.
>
> In other words, we should start with our *telos*, making our most crucial decisions on that basis, rather than hoping to consider our mission later. If we lose sight of the end and make our decisions about means on the basis of anything other than mission in the first place, we're lost.

---

[9] Bare, "Evaluation and the Sacred Bundle."

This is a good example of the need to know exactly what you have in your sacred core but also the need to treat it as sacred. It needs to be valued enough that it is measured, and because it is measured it will be valued more deeply in institutional decision-making.

Mission Implementation

A final way to think about implementing the institution's sacred core would be to ask and answer management expert Peter Drucker's "five most important questions you will ever ask about your organization."[10]

What is your mission?

Drucker's first question may seem obvious, but by now its importance for our purposes should be clear. Identifying the mission involves a clear mission statement but is much more than that. It is ensuring that the organization's mission is clear and communicated regularly at all levels of the institution so that anyone in the organization who is asked, "Why does this place exist?" will have a ready answer. Conversely, another way to put this would be to ask, "What would be lost if this place ceased to exist?" (not to mention, "Would our community notice if we ceased to exist?"). In addition, the related question to individual staff and faculty, "Why are YOU at this place?" is equally important, ensuring that the individual's personal mission is consistent with that of the organization to which that person has committed most of his or her waking hours for this season of their lives.

---

[10] Peter Drucker, *The Five Most Important Questions You Will Ever Ask About Your Organization* (San Francisco: Jossey-Bass, 2008).

Who is your customer?

Whom are you serving, or would like to be serving? For the Christian college/university, that is not as simple a question as it might appear on the surface. There are multiple constituents that we are called to serve, all at the same time. Students, of course, are the primary constituency whom we are serving, but in many cases, they are not the ones paying for the service—the parents are (often assisted by donors). Often the parents have a greater concern for mission fidelity than their students do, since they recognize the formative impact on their student during his or her time on your campus. We also serve alumni, many of whom desire an ongoing relationship with the school and are keenly interested that their alma mater not drift from its mission. We serve donors, another critical constituency, though it must be clear that the mission of the school is "not for sale." We also serve our communities, particularly the church and the academic guilds that our faculty populate, not to mention the community surrounding the campus, in which many of the school's employees live.

When it comes to students, we must first decide if we are serving Christian students exclusively or if we intend to serve a mixed population of students that are both Christian and non-Christian. We should recognize that the answer to that question deeply shapes the educational experience of students, the expectations of faculty, the way the curriculum is structured and taught, and the way faith is integrated into the curriculum. Some schools may have more of an emphasis on reaching students who have not yet begun a faith journey or who are in searching mode, while others require a statement of faith from incoming students and restrict the student body to explicitly Christian students. The mission emphasis is more on equipping for a life of service to God's kingdom and spiritual formation for these students. Of course, this also narrows the pool of potential students, but it can also be more attractive to Christian students and their parents, thereby making the school stand out as more distinctive than their competitors.

With reference to students, we also ask more specific questions about what groups of students we are serving. Do we serve a particular community? It may be that the school primarily serves students from a denomination, though it is unusual for a denominational school to restrict their student body to only those from that denomination. Our school may serve a particular ethnic community or a particular theological tradition. If the customer is a specific community, it is not normally exclusive to that community (exceptions would be Historically Black Colleges, or women's colleges, or military academies, for example), and the school must decide what its posture will be toward those coming in from outside that community. If those outside the community are allowed in, the school must be welcoming to those outside that primary community.

However, students are not the only constituency that our Christian college or university serves. Closely related to students, but with somewhat different interests, are parents of prospective and current students. They are asking questions about the return on investment for their student's educational costs—normally in the low to mid six figures for all expenses related to college. They are the ones pushing the question today, "Is college worth it?" This is particularly true at many of our Christian colleges and universities that do not have the prestige, facilities, depth of program offerings, or networking opportunities that bigger name institutions have. That is, the question they are asking is, "Is a Christian college education worth it, compared to other schools that their student could attend?"

Fortunately for Christian colleges, that is not the only question parents are asking. They are also interested in what will happen to their student's spiritual life during those formative college years. It is critically important to parents that the faith of their student be nurtured and that their student emerge from the college experience more confident in his or her faith than when he or she entered. In fact, that is often part of the recruiting pitch many Christian colleges give to the parents of prospective students. In addition, this is why parents sometimes grow disillusioned with a particular Christian college if the faith journey of their student does not meet their expectations. That is not to say that parents always expect that journey to be a smooth one, nor that students will not ask hard questions about their faith that reflect their attempt to own their faith for themselves. But in those cases in which students deconstruct their faith without fruitfully reconstructing it (hopefully under the guidance of a trusted advisor), parents will view the college as having failed in its primary mission.

Donors, both individuals/families and foundations, are another critically important constituency that ask even different questions of the institution to which they are giving. Like parents, donors (especially foundations) also ask questions about the return on their investment in the school, which is why they frequently give to specific projects with measurable outcomes. They are usually concerned with the mission fidelity of the school, and that is something that often is a source of pride for donors. Conversely, there are few issues that are more concerning to donors than the faithfulness of the school to its stated mission and values. For if they sense a shift in the school's priorities that they believe indicates a drift from the school's mission, they will stop giving until they are satisfied the school is headed in the right direction. In fact, they sometimes believe that the threat of their giving being discontinued, especially if they are significant and long-time donors, will help serve as a corrective to bring the school back on the right track. Donors want to be proud of the schools to which they give. They want to be assured the school is operating with integrity, is free from scandals that would be a source of embarrassment, and is actually doing the things to which they say they are committed.

Alumni are another constituency that also wants to be proud of their alma mater, though they may never give much financially or contribute much to the life of the campus after they graduate. But they do represent the school simply by virtue of their attendance there and having their university on their résumé. It is even better if they speak positively of their former collegiate experience as they interact with others. It is better still if they recommend the school to potential students and their families. Alumni are one of the primary sources of good will and positive public relations for the school. The questions they ask include, "Am I still proud of my school and having attended there?" and, "Did I have a good experience there that I am willing and able to tell others about?"

What does your customer value?

That is, why do students and parents tend to choose our particular school? What is the value proposition of our school that moves students to put down the money or incur the debt needed to fund their education or parents to write the checks for the education of their student? For many parents, their goals for their student are to secure the education necessary for a good job and career path, and perhaps, similar in importance is the goal of strengthening the faith of their student. They desire to see their student able to view their career through the lenses of their faith. For others, the goals may revolve around the well-traveled maxim, "Master, mission, mate"—that the college years are the time in which those three issues are settled and the trajectory in those three areas is set (though it is less likely than ever before that the "mate" issue is settled by graduation). Or it may be that the students/parents see the goal of graduating from as elite a school as possible as a means to the best paying and most prestigious job possible.

What are your results?

The most important result of any educational institution is its graduates, and this is sufficiently important that we will dedicate an entire chapter to it. It is helpful, however, to include a brief treatment of this question here. We must know that we are accomplishing our mission, but how? What evidence can the school give that it is delivering on the promises made to parents, students, and donors? One way of assessing the results is formally, through the various assessment mechanisms that accreditors mandate. In recent years, federal and state governments—the primary funding sources for higher education in the United States—are requiring schools to demonstrate that they are indeed having the impact on students that they have assured parents that they are. After all, government rightly demands a proper stewardship of the billions of dollars invested in higher education. They do not mandate what the mission of the school is, only that they are accomplishing what they are attempting to do.

Measuring results in a college or university is a different task than measuring results in a company, where sales, profit, and employee retention are the primary focal points and are easily empirically measurable. Assessment in higher education is much more complex since it involves results that have to do with character and spiritual formation—results that may not be evident for many years after graduation and are more difficult to measure empirically at any given point in time. In addition, even when it comes to measuring preparation for one's career, that may not be evident until several years after finishing college.

There are also informal ways of measuring what is important to a college or university. What a school values is often made evident through a variety of informal means. These can include the following:

- Which alumni are featured in university communications?
- Who is invited to give commencement addresses at graduation?
- Who receives honorary degrees from the school?
- Which students are highlighted for donor events?

The simple truth is that we become that which we highlight and celebrate. In addition, the funding priorities reveal the overall priorities of the school—which schools/departments are funded the most sufficiently, and which ones are underfunded, or in some cases, chronically underfunded?

Furthermore, the criteria for faculty promotion and tenure (if your school has tenure at all) are often very revealing of what is most important to a school. Is research and publication important to the school, or is it primarily a teaching institution (which, for many faculty is code for "do research and writing on your own time")? Are kinds of service incentivized and rewarded in the promotion criteria? These informal mechanisms will help the school identify and solidify their sacred core. The challenge is to ensure that the informal mechanisms are consistent with what the school says publicly about its mission and values.

What is your plan?

This is where strategic planning begins—once the mission and customer is identified and agreed upon. As the mission is executed with a strategic plan, it is critical to understand that the mission fidelity of the college/university is something that requires constant vigilance. It cannot be placed on "automatic pilot" and assumed that it will continue to flourish.

Mission fidelity requires clear mission communication and understanding throughout the school. But it is carried out by the personnel of the school, namely the faculty and cocurricular staff, who are those primarily entrusted with the education and formation of students. Of course, the senior leadership is responsible for setting the overall tone and guiding the mission. In addition, the leadership is tasked with reinforcing the mission with parents of students, donors, and alumni. It has long been assumed that it is the faculty who execute the mission on the ground with students, and to be sure, they play a pivotal role. However, it is increasingly recognized that the cocurricular staff is impacting students as significantly as the classroom faculty, if not more so. These influential staff members include those responsible for residential life on the campus, chapels, athletics, student organizations, and counseling/pastoral care of students. Vetting the cocurricular staff for mission fit is equally important for the health of the school as is vetting the faculty. This is why some schools require the cocurricular staff to affirm the school's doctrinal commitments in precisely the same way they require faculty to do so (the same may be required of senior leadership and board members as well). It is not difficult to envision multiple scenarios in which the curricular and cocurricular aspects of a student's experience are not coherent with each other, or even at odds. Take for example, a chapel speaker who models a hermeneutic or has a view of spiritual formation that is at serious variance with how the faculty teach hermeneutics/spiritual formation in their classrooms, and the speaker may even attempt to undermine such classroom efforts. Or take residential directors/dorm floor advisers who may influence students who have doubts or serious faith questions in ways that are not consistent with the school's theological commitments, given that students (in this case, RAs, who are students) are often not asked to commit to the same theological boundaries as the faculty and cocurricular staff. For those staff who do not have regular formational contact with students or donors (such as maintenance staff, food service employees, and financial affairs staff, for example), there can be more flexibility in what must be affirmed. Regardless of which staff members may be required to affirm the school's theological core, it would make sense to ensure that they realize what kind of institution employs them and that, at the least, they agree not to undermine or speak against the school's fundamental theological convictions.

Conclusion

So not every Christian college or university is alike. What distinguishes yours from the others, especially those with whom you compete for students and donors? What is your mission, specifically, beyond generic mission statements? Who are the constituents whom you are serving? What is the value proposition that makes your school stand out from the others?

What is your school's view of its founders and their vision for the school? If your school did not exist today, what would be the compelling reasons for founding such a school? What constitutes the sacred core of your school—those things that you must hold on to, no matter what? How will you know if you are staying true to that core and doing the things you claim to be doing? These are some of the pressing questions that any Christian institution of higher education must answer, and the answers will define what type of Christian college or university you are. In an age in which Christian colleges are becoming increasingly more alike, we would urge schools to craft a unique identity around faithfulness to its founders' intentions and, more importantly, fidelity to Christ and Scripture. Staying true to the mission of Christ-centered, biblically faithful education so that students are prepared to enter the adult world with their faith nurtured and robustly growing will make Christian colleges continue to be attractive to prospective students, their parents, and other supporters of the school.

Questions

1. What items would be in the "sacred bundle" of your institution? Identify several and reflect on why they are so significant and how they connect to important elements of the mission of your institution.
2. What threats to elements of your sacred core are you currently experiencing? How has your institution responded thus far, and what further steps do you believe need to be taken to assure mission fidelity?
3. What are some ways in which your institution measures and celebrates that which it values? Are there core values that go unmeasured and uncelebrated, and if so, why?

CHAPTER 4

WHAT IS A CHRISTIAN ACADEMIC DISCIPLINE?

It is vital that the university's mission informs the individual academic disciplines as they are taught at the university.

Imagine Professor Jones, a new faculty member at your Christian college/university. She is the newest addition to the department of sociology in your school of humanities and social sciences. She has spent the last six years in two different state universities—one pursuing her PhD and another in a postdoctoral fellowship. Her main area of research is the family and community dynamics of those who are in intractable poverty, and she is also involved in serving immigrant communities in her local area. She is grateful for her education, as she was exposed to many individuals and ideas that were new to her, and she feels well equipped for a career in research and teaching. She believes that her exposure to such a wide diversity of ideas will help prepare her students for the culture in which they will be living and making a living.

Professor Jones is also a committed Christian who attends a thriving local church regularly, is happily married to her husband, and is a great mom to her two young children. Her faith is one of the principal reasons she agreed to join the faculty of your school. She is thrilled to have secured not only an academic position but also one where she can be open about her faith with her students and colleagues. In her new faculty orientation, on several occasions, she heard about your school's emphasis on integration of faith and learning. She learned that integration is one of the hallmarks of the school and one that is promoted as a distinctive of the school to prospective students, their parents, potential faculty, and even prospective cocurricular staff. She remembers attending one of the orientation sessions for incoming students in her first year and hearing the president of the university proudly say that faculty are actually promoted in part for their work in integrating their faith and their discipline. It did not take long for her to realize that integration is a high value and one that is expected of all faculty regardless of their discipline.

Once classes began and she started teaching, she soon realized that her doctoral experience had not prepared her at all for what her students (and her dean) were expecting from her—a robust integration of Christian faith and sociology. She began to teach sociology the way it was taught to her—after all, that was all she knew. She had done all her graduate work in an environment that was either openly hostile to religious faith or viewed it as irrelevant to her academic work. She began to realize that she had never had any training in how to integrate her faith with her field, even though she very much wanted to do so. She had essentially "kept her head down" in her graduate work when it came to her faith and had neither the occasion nor any guidance in integration, not surprising when you consider the entirely secular, state university environment in which she did her graduate work. When she asked her colleagues about how they went about integration, she quickly realized that she was not alone in feeling underqualified to do something that her institution considered so important.

Integrative Thinking in Academic Disciplines

Professor Jones's story is not that unusual in many Christian colleges and universities. Men and women who come to our campuses from secular doctoral programs can underestimate how much they have absorbed from that setting—it is part of the air they breathe for four to six years in what is usually a very formative environment. In our view, overall, it is positive that Christian college and university faculty do their graduate work in these settings, since avoiding being educated in a Christian echo chamber is a good thing. In addition, it is beneficial for faculty while in their training to regularly engage with academics who come from entirely different worldviews, a trend that will hopefully continue throughout their careers.

It is not uncommon for Christian graduate students pursuing PhDs in secular universities to encounter hostility to their Christian faith, in part, for its decidedly un-postmodern metanarrative of a universal gospel and moral values that transcend time and culture. But more recently, this hostility takes a more virulent form when traditional views of marriage, sexuality, and abortion rights are the subjects. The discussion about these issues illustrates a new absolutism on many campuses with a corresponding increase in intolerance and canceling of those who hold such culturally heterodox views. As a result, Christian graduate students have many understandable reasons to "keep their heads down" when it comes to their faith, unintentionally perhaps, relegating their faith to the private sphere of their lives with little, if any, connection to their academic work. In addition, unless they are fortunate enough to have a professor during their study who is a Christian, they will get virtually nothing from their graduate work about how their faith should impact their academic work. But it may also be that their Christian professor is keeping his or her head down in their department, and may also have privatized faith in the course of his or her career. Our institutions need to be prepared for newly hired faculty to come with the *inclination* to meaningfully integrate their faith with their discipline, but without the *aptitude*. The opportunity to do integration well may be one of the main reasons they want to work at a Christian college or university, but in many cases, they are underprepared, since it is likely that no one taught them much about how to do this, nor did anyone model it for them.

Doing integration well also requires cooperation from faculty in biblical studies and theology. Integration is normally a team sport, not simply an individual accomplishment. Of course, if scholars in a specific discipline have sufficient biblical and theological education, they may be able to navigate the integrative landscape on their own. But simply having a vibrant faith is not enough. In most Christian universities, the level of biblical and theological sophistication among the faculty in the non-biblical/theological disciplines varies widely. In fact, at some Christian colleges and universities, upper-division undergraduates often have more theological education than most of the non-biblical/theological faculty on the campus. This may be particularly true for newer faculty who are fresh out of doctoral studies.

For the biblical and theological faculty, their exposure to disciplines outside their own is likely quite limited. One might assume that if you simply bring faculty from the sciences or humanities/social sciences together with faculty from Bible/theology, integration will somehow mystically occur. In fact, we would argue that another obstacle to doing integration well is the insular training, not only of the various academic disciplines but also of both biblical studies and theology. Here theologians and biblical studies faculty are often not much help in fostering integration among their colleagues, because they do not know much about, and often are not that interested in, any other discipline besides their own. Their guild demands specialization, and establishing an academic niche reinforces this. They are often very good in their field, but have been taught, especially those who have done doctoral work in Europe, to narrowly specialize. As a result, they typically do not think in integrative terms, and their plate is usually very full with teaching (especially with the elevated teaching loads in most Christian colleges and universities), research in their field, and service to their university (committee work, etc.). In addition, younger faculty usually have young families and may be doing other work to supplement their income, not uncommon in the early years of one's academic career. This perspective on the disciplines working together is important to realize given the temptation to assume that the faculty in Bible/theology have the answers for their colleagues in terms of how to do integration. Our experience is that the faculty in Bible/theology have as much to learn about integration as their colleagues in other disciplines. This requires that Bible/theology faculty seek to become better educated about the other disciplines that are present in his or her institution—not all of them, of course, but at least one other discipline. Of course, it is not necessary to become experts in another discipline but to know enough to be a good conversation partner with someone from that discipline. However, the deans and provost should understand that, for the theological faculty, this is a big ask that takes time and energy away from their own research and writing in their field. This is why schools must be prepared to incentivize faculty sufficient to motivate them to undertake such a task.

It may be that some fields are more intrinsically suited than others for this task. For example, my own field in ethics lends itself to cross-disciplinary work. Applied ethics demands an interdisciplinary focus. My (Scott's) experience in bioethics requires being conversant (not necessarily expertise) in five different areas—theology, philosophy, academic medicine, medical practitioners, and the law and legal literature. I did ICU rounds in several hospital settings to learn to connect with physicians and nurses, perused a handful of medical journals regularly, and spent hours in the law library on my surrogacy dissertation (tragically before LexisNexis was a thing!). In addition, I have spent years as a (very) informal theologian in residence in the business school, team-teaching business ethics and getting to know the business faculty. In business ethics there are similar areas that require being conversant—theology, philosophy, business literature, business practitioners, and the law.

It may also be the case that training in philosophy may provide more help to the integrative task than what is available to biblical scholars and theologians. Philosophers are sometimes more accustomed to something akin to integration because their discipline frequently addresses foundational issues in other disciplines as well. There are formally recognized fields of philosophy devoted to the underlying issues found in other academic disciplines. In fact, the Prentice Hall Foundations of Philosophy Series includes "philosophies of" no fewer than sixteen different academic disciplines.[1]

Much of the implementation of a Christian vision for a university takes place at the level of departments (or clusters of departments in a particular school). Departments, divisions, and schools play a crucial role in hiring, training, promoting, and granting tenure to faculty— the latter serves as an especially powerful means of communicating those things valued by the university. In addition, departments set the agenda for the curriculum that is the foundation for the hours of classroom interaction that students receive and will ultimately determine whether the institution will offer a distinctively Christian education. *It is vital that the university's mission informs the individual academic disciplines as they are taught at the university.* For this to happen, department chairs and deans must not only hire faculty who share the mission

---

[1] "Foundations of Philosophy (Prentice-Hall) - Book Series List," Publishing History, accessed December 26, 2023, https://www.publishinghistory.com /foundations-of-philosophy-prentice-hall.html.

(more on this later in chapter 5), but they must also create a climate of ongoing constructive Christian engagement with the content of the disciplines themselves.

Christian faculty in our institutions must live with a dynamic tension: the goodness of creation and the reality of sin. Sin means that we live in a fallen world, with cultures and institutions that have values and priorities at odds with a Christian worldview, so it is not difficult to fall into an oppositional mindset. The imagery of a garden mentioned in chapter 2 is helpful here as well. If the garden of secularism grows predominantly weeds, it is easy for Christian scholars to be preoccupied with killing weeds and never develop a Christian vision for the garden as a whole. Since all things are made by Christ and for Christ, they reflect the goodness of creation and exist under his lordship, and the Christian mind constantly asks what God intends for every aspect of creation and every arena of human endeavor. Faculty must generate this sort of a Christ-centered vision for their discipline and pass it along to their students.

So what exactly is meant by the term "integration"? Simply put, it is where general and special revelation intersect. That is, *integration is the task of identifying the touchpoints between one's discipline and one's Christian worldview and theology.* These may be places where there is mutual corroboration between the truths of Scripture and the truths of a specific discipline. Or conversely, there may be touchpoints that are not in concert, but in conflict. Either way, the overlapping concerns are a fertile ground for an integrative conversation.

Competing Models of Integration

The notion of integration is often misunderstood, frequently by well-intentioned faculty members who may never have seen good integration modeled for them. There is often a lack of clarity concerning the target. It seems that often faculty approach integration similar to life in the book of Judges, in which "everyone did what was right in their own eyes." The result is that faculty drift toward a set of default modes of integration that we have seen practiced in many university settings but which are not actually conducive to good integrative thinking.

Compartmentalization model

Compartmentalizing is not really a model of integration at all. It is a way to avoid integration. It is often the product of neglect. Some faculty members may have learned their Christianity from church or campus ministries and learned their academic discipline in a graduate program at a secular university. There was never really a point when either experience called on the other. Their minds have two separate, long-running tracks of education. They have been tacitly trained to think in two different compartments because their Christian education was ignorant of the questions and concerns of their secular education and vice versa.

Others compartmentalize with intention. They resist the idea that there should be an overlap between their Christianity and their academic training. There is a long history of this sort of thought within the Christian faith. Tertullian, for example, received an excellent secular education in Greek and Roman philosophy, but upon coming to Christ, he turned a very skeptical eye on the non-Christian learning:

> What indeed has Athens to do with Jerusalem? What concord is there between the Academy and the Church? what between heretics and Christians? . . . Away with all attempts to produce a mottled Christianity of Stoic, Platonic, and dialectic composition![2]

---

[2] Tertullian, *Tertullian On the Testimony of the Soul and On the "Prescription" of Heretics*, Early Church Classics, trans. T. Herbert Bindley (New York: E. S. Gorham, 1914), vii.

For Tertullian, the Academy and the Church were antagonistic domains—they were not only as distant as Athens and Jerusalem, they were at war with one another. To integrate these domains would merely produce a "mottled Christianity," corrupting knowledge, not completing it. Therefore, there is no positive integrative task. Nothing is gained by adding the findings of the philosophers to the writings of Scripture.

John Locke, many centuries later, adopted a similar posture with the opposite value system. He was concerned that faith would produce corrupted reasoning. He wanted sharp boundaries between faith and reason, noting that "the want whereof may possibly have been the cause, if not of great disorders, yet at least of great disputes, and perhaps mistakes in the world."[3] Locke feared that if "the provinces of faith and reason are not kept distinct by these boundaries, there will, in matters of religion, be no room for reason at all."[4] For him, reason grounded in sense perceptions gave the clearest knowledge. Faith grounded in divine revelation was an uncertain foundation for knowledge at best.

Compartmentalization readily falls prey to a sharp divide between sacred and secular concerns. It also prompts the question as to why one needs a Christian university at all. As was seen in chapter 2, there are many unique contributions that Christian thought makes to higher education, and compartmentalizing ignores or neglects these contributions.

Ministry model

In this case, there is an active intent to integrate faith and learning, but the task is viewed mainly as inserting the practices of religious faith into nonreligious contexts. It means marketplace ministries where business-persons hold evangelistic luncheons or have Bible study groups in the

---

[3] John Locke, *Essay Concerning Human Understanding* (Oxford: Oxford University Press, 1975), iv.18.1.

[4] Locke, iv.16.11.

company cafeteria. It means sharing your faith in your classroom or with your clients or with your patients. It can include earning money through traditional business practices as long as that money is given to the church or to missions so that the gospel is advanced. This mindset is common among faculty in part because it is so common in the churches they attend. Evangelical churches often want their members to integrate their faith into their workplace by evangelizing their coworkers, neighbors, and friends or by inviting them to church. The value of doing such things should not be denied, but this way of thinking blinds us to the intrinsic value of work that glorifies God and tangibly fulfills the command to love our neighbor. It reinforces the idea that only clergy really have a calling that serves God—everyone else just has a job.

Whether in the academy or the workplace, it is a profound failure of our theological imagination when we can only see Christian value in things that look like an aspect of a church service. Squeezing Jesus into everything on "spiritual" terms can make it seem like beauty in the arts, or truth in the hard sciences, or goodness in a work of literature is not good on its own; these are only instrumental goods that can be used as a springboard to spiritual things, which are the "real" goods. The problem with the ministry model of integration is not what it does (evangelism and Bible studies are good things to do) but what it leaves undone—namely, applying the Christian faith to all our daily activities and responsibilities.

To help illustrate why this matters, imagine you are a pastor in Detroit in the early 1900s. One Sunday morning you see Henry Ford walk into the back of your church. You give an altar call at the end of the service, and much to your astonishment, he comes forward to receive Christ. You are thrilled! The next morning you hear a knock on your door at the church office, and you open the door to see Henry Ford standing there. He tells you he was serious about his profession of faith and wants to know exactly what he should do now. What would you say? Tithe to the church? Lead a Bible study at work? Join the elders board? Evangelize his workers? Obviously, these are all good things to do, but notice that these questions miss his greatest stewardship entirely. They do not even touch on the way he runs his company. He is the CEO of a factory that employs fifty thousand workers. If a disciple is meant to see all he or she owns as a stewardship from God, Henry Ford might want to think about the working conditions in his factory, the pay of his workers, and the welfare of the community of which his factories are a part. The conditions of industrial workers were a major social problem in the early 1900s. Pope Pius XI put it well when he said that God ordained work "for the good at once of man's body and soul, [but work] is being everywhere changed into an instrument of perversion; for dead matter comes forth from the factory ennobled, while men there are corrupted and degraded."[5]

As a pastor, you would not be able to tell Henry Ford how to run his factory—you simply do not know enough about factories. However, you do know enough about theology to know that everything we do matters to Jesus and that Henry Ford should feel responsible to put his substantial skills, resources, and energy into discovering ways in which he could make his factory increasingly conducive to human flourishing rather than human degradation. He needs to make a profit, and he also needs to see his employees as people made in the image of God and over whom God has appointed him as a leader and employer. The important thing is that you encourage him to ask and answer different sorts of questions about his factory than those that had probably been in his mind before he became a Christian.

These same issues just described in a church setting apply equally well in the academic setting. Take the business school as an example. If all that matters is using business as a platform for living out one's faith

---

[5] Pope Pius XI, "Quadragesimo Anno," The Holy See, May 15, 1931, https://www.vatican.va/content/pius-xi/en/encyclicals/documents/hf_p-xi _enc_19310515_quadragesimo-anno.html.

(including verbally sharing the gospel when possible and appropriate) or using the financial success of one's business as the "supply line" for the "front lines" of church ministry and missions, the vision for business in and of itself will be identical to that which will be taught in a secular school. The only difference will be the use to which profits are put. The assumption underlying this model is that the work that is important to God is evangelism, local churches, and missions. This sets up an unbiblical hierarchy of callings that also neglects what the businessperson does with the majority of his or her time. Rarely does this model include the actual work itself in which the businessperson is engaged. That is, the businessperson is engaged in "ministry" in the workplace, *but only when not doing his or her job.* But the Bible is quite clear that the work itself is part of a person's service to God (Col 3:23–24). In this model, the faculty member sees the "ministry" of his or her classroom as something unrelated to the content of the course he or she is teaching.[6]

Cultural critique model

A third model of integration that is common among faculty and church members alike is the cultural critique model. In this case, one realizes that the gospel really does have implications for all of human life. Human culture-making is exactly an act of "doing something with the world," so Christians should be actively concerned about what our culture is doing. This concern is expressed in critically examining our modern culture and speaking up when it does things that are not pleasing to God. For some it might mean protesting a movie or boycotting a product or writing a Congress member or joining a school board.

---

[6] For further discussion of the sacred-secular dichotomy and its application to the concept of vocation, see Kenman L. Wong and Scott B. Rae, *Business for the Common Good: A Christian Vision for the Marketplace* (Downers Grove: IVP Academic, 2012), chaps. 1–3.

The common element here is not a particular political orientation but rather a posture toward culture—the posture of a referee. Referees are not players. They are the people who watch the players and blow the whistle when they do something wrong.

Since there are plenty of things wrong with our culture, there is no denying the need for refereeing, but there are some unintended side effects of adopting this posture. First, referees are not viewed favorably by most people. At best, they are viewed as a necessary evil. At worst, they are an impediment to enjoying a game. I (Rick) often ask my students if they played high school or college sports and discover that a large number have. I then ask how many of these athletes had their lives impacted by a coach or fellow player, and almost everyone will raise their hand. Finally, I ask if they have had their life impacted by a referee—almost no one puts up their hand, and if they do, they always tell a negative story. Referees may be necessary, but they are not seen as positive contributors. If Christians view cultural engagement as refereeing culture, we will likely be contributing to a very negative view of Christianity.

Another problem with the cultural critique model is related to a lack of vision. We have already mentioned Abraham Kuyper's famous cry that "there is not one square inch over which Jesus does not cry, 'Mine!'" But being global in one's claims requires one to be positive in one's vision. There is no point in demanding the entire world if you have not figured out what to do with it once you get it. Christians may know what to do with a church, but what do we do with a mountain, a mill, or a midge fly? And for that matter, do we know what to do with a movie or a mural? Many commentators in the past century have lamented that Christians have abandoned countless spheres of human culture and neglected the created order as well. Perhaps we are preoccupied with "spiritual matters," and perhaps not, but part of why secular thinking dominates so many fields is that sacred thinking has spent so little time there.

What is needed is a clear vision of a Christian aspect of the particular part of the created order under consideration. It is good to identify the ways in which an aspect of the created order or a sphere of human endeavor has been distorted by the fall, corrupted by the world, or exploited for the purposes of Satan. This must be followed up, however, by asking what that aspect of the created order or that sphere of human endeavor would look like if it were once again subject to the lordship of Christ and were awaiting his return.

Cultural participation model

This final model takes up the challenge of casting a positive vision for the garden of human culture, and *it is the model that we highly recommend*. It encourages Christians to cultivate a Christian imagination for academic disciplines and cultural activities. It approaches culture as a player or a coach rather than as a referee. It should be noted that players and coaches still honor the rules of the game—otherwise they will likely lose. Their preoccupation, however, is with strategies for playing the game.

There is a long history of Christians adopting this posture toward culture. Christians have not just written books; they have created genres. Augustine wrote the Western world's first autobiography, and in so doing he put forward a view of the individual human soul that was compelling enough to serve as the focus for an entire, lengthy work of literature. His work created autobiography as a genre of literature and also opened a new vista for the writing of biographies as well. He also pioneered historiography when he wrote *The City of God*. Augustine was not preoccupied with critiquing Roman authors of his day; rather, he was creating new and enduring cultural goods.

In more recent memory, J. R. R. Tolkien almost single-handedly created the modern genre of fantasy literature. It proved to be such an enduring cultural good that countless other authors, secular and

Christian alike, have imitated him and made fantasy literature one of the most popular genres in book sales. Boyle, Kepler, Pascal, and many other early modern scientists were driven by a desire to know and understand God's created order by means of systematic study and mathematical description. Roger Williams pioneered modern notions of political pluralism, freedom of conscience, and the separation of church and state. In all these cases, Christians did not imitate existing cultural goods but pioneered new ones. They did not critique; they created. They were not referees; they were players. But most of all, they were captured by a Christian imagination for every aspect of the created order and every sphere of human endeavor. They had a faith that was fully integrated and committed to stewarding all things toward the glory of Christ.

Before leaving this discussion, we should also identify some cheap substitutes for the real thing when it comes to integration. They are not necessarily fully developed "models" of integration but rather techniques that we can easily drift into that create the impression of integrative thinking when little or no integrative thinking has actually been done. There is the "devotional before class" substitute, in which the professor makes a good-faith attempt to nurture the spiritual lives of his or her students, but the activity toward this end is a devotional unrelated to the actual content of the class material. The class is viewed as actually beginning when the devotional time is complete. This reinforces the notion that the spiritual and academic sides of life are separate and distinct, though both the devotional time and prayer time can be very meaningful to students. In addition, there is the "Christmas tree" substitute, in which Bible verses are hung, figuratively speaking, on a preexisting syllabus, with no noticeable change in the actual content of what is being taught. Further, there is the "hermit crab" substitute, which assumes the shell of the existing aspect of culture without questioning it and then packs the inside full of "Christian" content. For example, one might teach the framework of the four personality types (sanguine, choleric, phlegmatic, melancholic) by identifying each with a biblical person (Paul or Peter or Timothy or Jeremiah). The biblical illustrations create the illusion that the structure itself is biblical, but it really is not. It may even lead to unbiblical thinking, such as when a person is rude or bossy toward others and excuses that by saying that they have the choleric personality type. Similar things are commonly done with the enneagram. The main point here is not that the personality types or the enneagram is evil or anti-biblical, it is just that the professor baptizes an existing structure by providing a set of verses or a biblical illustration and thereby exempts it from careful and critical examination by a Christian worldview. These substitutes are often viewed as "add-ons" to the course content but do not substantively change anything about the course itself. As one dean put it to us, "If you view integration simply as an add-on, you don't understand our mission."

Topics for Integrative Conversations

Although integrative thinking about an academic discipline is essential to Christian higher education, it is almost never taught in the graduate programs that train most of our Christian faculty. If it is learned at all, it will be learned by intentional effort—either the efforts of a highly motivated faculty member or the efforts of a Christian university structuring it into the continuing education and promotion requirements for their faculty. Simply stating the desire that faculty integrate a deeply Christian worldview into all their teaching is insufficient. A single chapter in a book of this length is insufficient to remedy this glaring shortfall; however, it is possible to give a hint at the kinds of *conversation topics and questions* that might contribute to such thinking.

Content

First, and most obviously, there are many cases in which the findings of academic study of culture and creation clearly overlap with biblical teaching. For example, the Bible talks about emotions, and so does the academic discipline of psychology. The same is true for a concept like personal identity. Positive psychology has studied character qualities like altruistic love, generosity, grace, humility, forgiveness, and thankfulness. All these topics have substantial biblical teaching associated with them. If integration of faith and learning involves bringing together the findings of both general and special revelation, all these topics would be natural places to do it. In the case of positive psychology, for example, this might involve comparing and contrasting the definition of love or forgiveness within the academic discipline of psychology with the biblical understanding of these concepts. One would likely identify areas where the concepts are congruent with one another, other areas where they are complementary but different, and still other areas of apparent conflict. In all these cases, one finds a starting point for an integrative conversation.

Integrative conversations can also involve a subject like poverty, which is not confined to a particular academic discipline but rather is an issue of general human concern. Scripture has a lot to say about poverty, but the topic is also studied in social sciences such as sociology, political science, and economics. Furthermore, novels such as *Great Expectations, The Grapes of Wrath,* and *Les Misérables,* as well as movies such as *Parasite, The Pursuit of Happyness,* and *City of God* all offer penetrating insights into poverty. They offer a glimpse at the experience not only of poverty but also of wealth, and at the social dynamics of human relationships that arise when there are large economic gaps in a society. Within our own university, we developed a January-term class that studied social issues such as poverty and many others by means of a combination of novels and films, relevant academic disciplines, and biblical and theological reflection. The class was taught for several years by a group of faculty from a wide variety of academic disciplines. Each nine-hour day focused on a book that had been made into a movie. Professors used their different expertise to address important issues related to the films by means of lecture and discussion, then the movie was shown, and immediately afterward we had a lengthy discussion about the movie and its points of intersection with the academic disciplines and biblical and theological issues. These classes remain some of the best experiences of integrative teaching in my (Rick's) career.

But of course, there are academic disciplines in which it is a lot harder to find overlapping content. For example, in disciplines like accounting or physics or chemistry, the topics addressed are technical in nature and have little apparent connection with Scripture. The Bible does not discuss double-entry accounting systems, the valence shell electron pair repulsion theory, or quantum electrodynamics. But just because there is little or no overlapping content, that does not mean there is no room for an integrative conversation. Let us consider at least four other points of contact one might use to frame an integrative conversation: goals, assumptions, methodologies, and theories (or narratives).

Goals

We have already spent a substantial amount of time talking about goals in this book. Our reflections on the university itself—its goals and purpose for being—actually models an integrative conversation. Notice that we have spent time looking at both secular and Christian thinkers. Notice, as well, that there is a very robust conversation going on among these thinkers. It is not a simple conversation that quickly arrives at a conclusion everyone shares. Anthony Kronman worries that the university has sold its birthright by disengaging from the "big questions" of the meaning of life. Stanley Fish, with equal zeal and eloquence, argues that the university never should have been concerned about such questions to being with. It is also clear that many Christian thinkers like Newman, Lewis, and Berry are concerned not just with the Christian university but with the university itself. They bring the Christian mind to bear on what the role of a university is in society. They are modeling a Christian mind that is not confined to internal Christian concerns but rather the entire scope of creation and human culture. Goals are a terrific springboard for integrative conversation.

Assumptions

All academic disciplines have certain assumptions built into them. Just like goals, many of these assumptions are hidden or unquestioned, and therefore, bringing them out for inspection can lead to a productive integrative conversation. One example of this comes from a sociology textbook, describing essential assumptions of the discipline.

> Fundamental to our view is the assumption that the universe has no intrinsic meaning—it is, at bottom, absurd—and the task of the sociologist is to discover the various imputed or fabricated meanings constructed by people in society. . . . Meaningless produces terror. And terror must be dissipated by participating in, and believing in, collective fictions.[7]

To start an integrative conversation, a person might question the assumption that the universe is basically meaningless. It is easy for a Christian to say that a human life or the universe itself has meaning because of God, but how exactly does that work? How does God's existence serve to refute the claims of a secular scholar who is making the assertions found in the quote above? Raising issues like this will deepen a student's understanding both of God and of the academic

---

[7] Harvey A. Farberman and Erich Goode, *Social Reality*, Prentice-Hall Sociology Series (Englewood Cliffs, NJ: Prentice-Hall, 1973), 2.

discipline. But there are a lot of other issues one might discuss. For example, one might consider the consequences of this assumption for sociology. If one assumes not only that there is no God, but that the universe is inherently meaningless, and that all meaning is simply a social construct or a fabrication, what does this blind a person to? What research questions are never asked? What possible solutions to social problems are never considered? What gaps occur in the research of a discipline that is shaped by an assumption like this? This is an invitation for an integrative conversation as well, and it would be a conversation that addresses matters important to any practitioner of that academic discipline—not just those who are Christians.

Methodologies

Academic disciplines have a particular way of going about their work—the tools of the trade, so to speak. They adopt a particular methodology or methodologies. To use one famous example from the natural sciences, we often talk about "methodological naturalism." In other words, whatever one believes about the natural and the supernatural realms, as a matter of methodology, a scientist should check his or her supernatural beliefs at the door. Scientific studies must be pursued in a methodologically naturalistic way. Only things that can be observed in nature should be treated (addressed, studied) in the laboratory. Let me share a quote from the American Geological Society that captures this very nicely: "Natural processes are sufficient to explain or account for natural phenomenon or events. In other words, scientists must explain the natural in terms of the natural, and not the supernatural, which, lacking any independent evidence, is not falsifiable, and therefore not science."[8] It

---

[8] Christine McLelland, "The Nature of Science and the Scientific Method" (Boulder, CO: The Geological Society of America, n.d.), 1, https://rock .geosociety.org/net/documents/gsa/geoteachers/NatureScience.pdf.

is clear from that quotation that geological science is meant to adopt a naturalistic methodology.

Reflecting on methodology is a natural starting point for an integrative conversation. Consider Sir Arthur Eddington's description of the theoretical problems caused by methodological choices.[9] He asks one to imagine an ichthyologist who drops a net into the ocean in search of fish, and then, upon surveying his catch, he proceeds to make two generalizations: (1) no sea creature is less than two inches long, and (2) all sea creatures have gills. Both are true of his catch, and he repeats his experiment again and again, gaining ever more confidence in his conclusion. In this story, Eddington notes, the catch represents a body of knowledge that could be found in any physical science, and the net represents the sensory and intellectual apparatus used in obtaining it. He then imagines an onlooker who complains that the conclusion is wrong, not because of the interpretation of the data, but because of the *methodology* adopted. The methodological problem lies with the net that has two-inch holes, so it cannot catch fish smaller than two inches. Eddington offers the following response from the high-minded scientist:

> The ichthyologist dismisses this objection contemptuously. "Anything uncatchable by my net is *ipso facto* outside the scope of ichthyological knowledge, and is not part of the kingdom of fishes which has been defined as the theme of ichthyological knowledge. **In short, what my net can't catch isn't fish.**" Or— to translate the analogy—"If you are not simply guessing, you are claiming a knowledge of the physical universe discovered in some other way than by the methods of physical science, and

---

[9] Arthur Eddington, *The Philosophy of Physical Science* (Cambridge, MA: Cambridge University Press, 1949), 17, http://archive.org/details/in.ernet.dli .2015.425432.

admittedly unverifiable by such methods. You are a metaphysi-
cian. Bah!"[10]

The story is both amusing and instructive. It is not a refutation
of methodological naturalism, and it does not prove that naturalistic
assumptions fail to produce knowledge. The important point he makes
is that naturalistic assumptions fail to exhaust knowledge. They limit
what can be discovered and discussed within the domain in which they
reign supreme.

Beyond the concerns that Eddington identifies, one further concern must be mentioned. When one adopts a methodology at the outset, that must be remembered when it comes time to draw conclusions.
Failing to do this has been a major concern in many sciences, at least
on the part of Christian commentators. If you assume methodological naturalism at the outset, then you cannot make a conclusion about
the nonexistence of God at the end of the process. You have adopted
a methodology that is explicitly designed to ignore divine causation
by deciding at the start that nothing other than a natural cause counts
when doing science. This may or may not lead to good science, but
it certainly leads to limited science—a science with methodological
boundaries. When we read comments by evolutionary scientists or
cosmologists reaching conclusions about the nonexistence of God or
the absence of divine activity, we need to remind ourselves that those
were conclusions that were guaranteed by the methodologies adopted
at the outset of the study.

Economics also offers a good example of the importance of integrative conversations—in this case regarding both assumptions and
methodology. As theologian Stanley Hauerwas notes:

Economics [is] a discipline currently dominated by mathematical models and rational-choice theories. Those theories may

---

[10] Eddington, 16. Emphasis added.

have some utility (to use an economic expression), but they also may entail anthropological assumptions that a Christian cannot accept. You will not be in a position even to see the problem, much less address it, if you let your intellectual life be defined by your discipline.[11]

Hauerwas identifies both assumptions (in this case anthropological) and methodologies (in this case mathematical modeling and rational choice theory) and prods his readers to avoid letting their intellectual horizons be limited to the boundaries of their disciplines. To unpack the example of economics more fully, it *assumes* that all human value can somehow be reduced to monetary values that are amenable to a *methodology* of mathematical modeling. By means of such models, one can track the value of current monetary transactions and perhaps predict future ones. The problem is that there are certain things that do not reduce very well to a monetary value. What is the worth of a baby? Of a person's human dignity? Such things are without a price. But in economics, if something does not have a price, it is methodologically orphaned; there is no place for it in the mathematical model. If it does not count in the calculation, instead of becoming priceless, it becomes worthless in the sense that its worth fails to register. One then wonders how to implement and establish economic policy that captures what is valuable to human beings but which is not easily reduced to monetary value. This is a fitting place for an integrative conversation.

Theories and narratives

Although the postmodern world is, by definition, skeptical toward metanarratives, the fact remains that the academic disciplines are often

---

[11] Stanley Hauerwas, "Go with God," First Things, November 2010, https://www.firstthings.com/article/2010/10/go-with-god.

formed by narratives, and many of these narratives span a broad range of academic disciplines. In other words, they really do become meta-narratives. For example, Marxism is a theory and a narrative about the way the world works. It has spread across many different academic disciplines. It begins with narrowly economic questions about the ownership of the means of production. But it then expands to the world of culture and ideas, which it sees as a superstructure propped up by the foundation of means of production. Marx also reshapes our understanding of sociology and plays a dominant role of literary criticism. One finds Marxism expressed in political theory, philosophy, and many other academic disciplines. Clearly, Marxism becomes a metanarrative that spreads across vast swaths of the university. It is very helpful to bring such a narrative into conversation with its scriptural counterpart, such as the narrative of the kingdom of God. One can examine how these narratives push and pull against one another, giving very different perspectives on human nature, the human plight, and the destiny of human history.

Evolution is similar to Marxism in that it has also become a very expansive narrative. Beginning with zoological and biological concerns, it was very quickly applied to social issues and racial differences. Then it spread to religious thinking that now includes the so-called religious evolution of polytheism to monotheism. Today you can find evolutionary psychology, evolutionary chemistry, and evolutionary economics. It has spread to almost every academic discipline as a framing device. Again, this is not an inherent indictment of the academic disciplines or a disproof of the theories in question. Rather, it is a reminder that these theories and narratives need to be treated as such and not as iron-clad facts or unquestionable assumptions. In fact, they are invitations to an integrative conversation that brings these narratives into discussion with the biblical narrative—including overarching themes like kingdom, covenant, and the biblical plotline of creation, fall, redemption, and consummation.

In summary, it is important that Christian scholars diversify the kinds of integrative conversations they see arising from their disciplines. Conversations about overlapping content are easy and natural, but they only make up a small portion of the opportunities for the integration of faith and learning within an academic discipline.

Spiritual formation

So far, our discussion of integration has focused mostly on the non-biblical/theological disciplines, with the goal of finding the relevant touchpoints between the specific disciplines and the elements of a Christian worldview. The object of discussion has been the things that a particular academic discipline investigates and the task of developing a distinctively Christian view of these things. However, this works in the opposite way as well. A final way to develop one's thinking about integration is to see our professional disciplines as a particular context in which we live our Christian lives and to investigate the ways in which that context offers creative opportunities and challenges for our spiritual formation. This is particularly important in the disciplines of Bible and theology, where learning and study should never be merely academic but should apply the biblical text or point of theology to the student's spiritual life and formation, but it should not be confined to the Bible and theology, because the spiritual formation of students is the job of all faculty, regardless of one's discipline.

Faculty in the various non-biblical/theological fields should be encouraged to apply insights from their field to the spiritual lives of their students when they can. For example, if human beings are made in the image of God, that has much to say about how persons should be treated that applies directly to how businesses treat their employees, how governments and communities treat migrants to their countries, or how persons are more than the sum of their economic self-interests. Of course, the importance of all the curriculum contributing to the student's spiritual formation does not mean that it should be any less rigorous, nor should it turn the course into a semester-long Bible conference. And of course, some disciplines lend themselves to this kind of application more than others. For example, almost all business schools address business ethics. But in most business schools (including the one where I [Scott] was a TA for three semesters as a doctoral student), that is where the course begins and ends. At a Christian school, there is more that can be done. My co-teacher and I devote the final two weeks of the course to the moral and spiritual development of the student. We focus on two primary areas of business that both nurture and reveal a person's character—how they handle money and how they relate to power. We also make regular observations throughout the course about how our Christian worldview impacts how we view ethics; how virtue, trustworthiness, and character are important for leadership in business; and how employees are treated, among other touchpoints. But we also spend concentrated time in the concluding weeks of the course focused intently on individual character formation, through the lenses of money and power.

However, students studying in courses in biblical studies and theology should expect that their course material regularly have something meaningful to say about their spiritual formation. The study of the biblical text, however technical, should not be limited to the fine points of exegesis or the historical and cultural background to the text under consideration. Students should also be challenged to think about how the text at hand can shape their spiritual lives. Even in survey courses of the Old and New Testament, the message of individual books of the Bible can and should be related to the spiritual formation of students, which adds to the richness of the material as opposed to taking away from its rigor. Similarly, in theology, the major doctrines—regardless of their fine distinctions, historical development, and points of controversy (most of which are very important)—can and should be routinely related to the students' spiritual lives. This can and should be some of the most transformative, challenging, and interesting parts of our teaching. If the Bible and theology are meant to do more than increase our students' information but to transform their lives, then this kind of integration of the Bible and theology should be one of the primary arenas in which our students find their spiritual formation nurtured. Having come to faith in Young Life, where founder Jim Rayburn's motto was, "It's a sin to bore a kid with the gospel,"[12] we would take that a step further to say, as we have repeatedly told our current and prospective faculty, "It's a sin to bore a student with the Bible and theology."

Conclusion

Becoming equipped to do integration consistently and well requires more than simply attending a seminar or two on the subject or team-teaching a course with someone from another discipline. Learning to do rigorous, deep, and inspiring integration is a lifelong task—a marathon, not a sprint! It often takes many years of interdisciplinary conversation, team-teaching, study, and research to become proficient at this. Consider this narrative, which, in our view, is not atypical among Christian college and university faculty.

> I received my baccalaureate education in English Literature at Wheaton College, Wheaton, Illinois, and felt myself well equipped to enter a secular university graduate program. However, no formal educational experience can effectively prepare a person for the challenges of living cross-culturally. Entering the department of anthropology at the University of Pittsburgh, I found only one person sympathetic to my Christian experience, a fellow graduate student whose mother had been

---

[12] This mirrors the title of Char Meredith, *It's a Sin to Bore a Kid: The Story of Young Life* (Waco, TX: Word Books, 1978).

a follower of Bishop Fulton Sheen. The faculty stated openly and unequivocally that religious commitments had no place in the science of society, although religious beliefs and experience were a legitimate subject for research by anthropologists. A few of the faculty expressed open hostility toward Christianity. During my three years of graduate education I learned to be very quiet about my Christian faith, and very selective about whom I might share privately my personal beliefs.

Perhaps more importantly, my PhD mentor told me gently, as part of his professional support, that my religious background was irrelevant to my professional life, and that he intended to guide me to become the best anthropologist I could be. It was clear that religion and faith had nothing to do with this mission. After a few traumatic experiences, one in particular with physical anthropology, I accepted the naturalist and evolutionary paradigm as the only one acceptable in the profession for the study of human life and culture. I left the University of Pittsburgh to launch my teaching career in a college of the State University of New York, committed, more or less, to the doctrines of human and cultural evolution as taught to me by my professors.

In the early years of my academic tenure in SUNY I parked my Christianity quietly in a closet and ignored this aspect of my personal history and life. In this setting all of my colleagues were non-Christian and once again religion was a subject to be studied, but certainly not a life to be lived. For fifteen years I nurtured habits as a scholar/teacher in the department of anthropology, conducting research, writing, teaching without reference to my Christian heritage or faith.

My wife and I attended the Summer Institute of Linguistics in 1975, where I met two men, Marvin K. Mayers and William Merrifield, both competent anthropologists and committed Christians. Our conversations led to my reconsideration of the Christian faith, and a renewed commitment to the Lord Jesus Christ.

When I returned to the State University of New York I faced the dilemma of how to nurture this renewed Christian faith and continue my professional relationships in anthropology. I resolved to keep my Christian faith private and continue my professional relationships as they had been before, unchanged.

When invited to join the faculty of Biola University in 1983, I came thoroughly indoctrinated in the naturalism and empirical perspectives of secular anthropology. For nearly two decades I had effectively compartmentalized my life so that my faith had nothing to do with my professional practice. Suddenly in a Christian institution students and colleagues expected me to integrate my faith and my academic discipline. Habits of 20 years are not easily broken. My first few years at Biola were somewhat rocky for my students and for me. These students had obvious expectations about what they should be getting in a Christian college and at times I did not fill those expectations. One of my students complained bitterly that she had left a community college and came to Biola specifically to avoid the kind of teaching that I offered in Introductory Anthropology. Encouraging her to bear with me, I assured her of my personal commitment to the Lord Jesus Christ and promised that she would find perspectives in my class not taught at the community college.

At that time I was hard pressed to explain what it meant to teach from a Christian perspective and worldview.

At about the same time the dean of the School of Intercultural Studies, Dr. Marvin K. Mayers, arranged for monthly meetings between our faculty and the faculty of the Talbot School of Theology. Over the next two years we gathered for monthly dialogue. Individuals in each school prepared and presented papers for discussion by the group. I cannot speak for the others, but the substantive change in my thinking occurred over the three years which followed. By the end of my fourth year at Biola I had experienced a significant paradigm shift in my thinking about culture and anthropological research. Grappling with the fact that my anthropological presuppositions frequently contradicted my understanding of scriptures, I had to decide my priorities for each of source of knowledge.

No longer comfortable with the compartmentalization that had characterized my career, and bringing these two fields together, I reached the conclusion that my anthropology had to be redefined in reference to my Christian faith. I began to rethink my approach to the field of anthropology from this theological point of view. Everything I have written in subsequent years has been profoundly influenced by this paradigm shift. The teaching in all of my courses has taken a substantive new direction. After a five-year journey I had finally begun the task of integrating my faith and my academic discipline and teaching the subject of social anthropology from a Christian perspective and worldview.[13]

Questions

1. How does your school currently equip faculty to better integrate their faith and their specific academic disciplines? What, if anything, does your school offer to new faculty about integration as part of their orientation?
2. What faculty members or classroom experiences reflect the sort of integration that your school aspires to?

---

[13] Sherwood Lingenfelter, "The Integration of Christian Faith and Academic Scholarship: A Case Study of Biola University, 1992–95," (unpublished paper prepared for Fieldstead Foundation, 2018), 14–17.

3. How are the biblical studies/theology faculty encouraged/incentivized to become good conversation partners with faculty in other disciplines?
4. Which of the models of integration presented in this chapter best exemplifies your institution's approach to integration?
5. What mechanisms do you have in place for assessing and celebrating good integration of faith and learning?

CHAPTER 5

CREATING AND MAINTAINING A CULTURE OF MISSION FIDELITY

*It is critical that everyone involved in hiring recognize
that mission fidelity is everyone's business.*

Clarifying the mission of Christian higher education is necessary but not sufficient to ensure mission fidelity. Every school must also create institutional structures that both promote and reward faithfulness to the university's mission, thereby creating a culture that is conducive to missional commitment. Requirements such as signing doctrinal statements or membership in a particular church or denomination are not enough. Recruitment of students, hiring of faculty and cocurricular staff, institutional messaging, financial incentives and integrity, and human resource policies all must be arranged to reflect the overriding missional priorities of the school. The larger the college or university, the more coordination this takes to ensure that everyone is "rowing in the same direction" and not inadvertently, or intentionally, working at cross purposes. This chapter is aimed at those academic and cocurricular leaders, the ones who are primarily responsible for establishing and maintaining a culture conducive to missional faithfulness. But we also recognize that maintaining such a culture is that everyone's business and that everyone in the institution has a stake in ensuring that this kind of culture is nurtured.

Mission Ownership

To begin this discussion, it will be helpful to think a bit more closely about mission ownership. Mission ownership goes far beyond merely having a written mission statement; it is much more a matter of knowing what a mission statement looks like when it is unpacked and expressed in the life of your college or university. Here is a short list of elements that contribute to mission ownership:

Knowing the mission: Knowing the mission means being able to identify the distinguishing features of the mission in a way that is more akin to knowing a person than to knowing a fact. Memorizing the mission statement of your university is a good place to start, but much more important is the ability to recognize mission success in the lives of those who make up your community. It means you have an idea of what mission fidelity and mission drift would look like in the life of a student, faculty member, staff member, board member, or donor.

Inspired by the mission: If you own the mission, it means that the mission is the sort of thing that gets you out of bed in the morning. It is not merely that you can accurately describe the mission but that when you are describing it, you also feel moved by it. It ignites your passions, energizes your efforts, and sparks your dreams.

Aligned by the mission: Owning the mission means that you understand your job and institutional responsibilities in a mission-related way. You do not just know your job description and reporting relationships; you know how what you are doing contributes to the missional success of the university. You find your mission embedded in your everyday activities and see others around you pulling together on that same mission.

Implementing the mission: The mission, understood in the depth we have described here, demands tangible expression—it shouts for it. Institutional activities need to be intentionally mission-shaped. Programs are planned, executed, assessed, and then revised by their effectiveness in moving the mission forward. Upon revision, they are re-implemented, and the process begins all over again. So the mission is not static, nor is it merely descriptive; it is directive and dynamic.

Celebrating the mission: Mission fulfillment is a cause for recognition, reward, and celebration. Public events—all university events—should celebrate missional achievements. Convocation messages, graduation speakers, awards, promotional material, institutional magazines, and websites should all be identifying and celebrating mission success.

Signs of Mission Drift

One important question for Christian colleges and universities to ask themselves regularly has to do with the indicators that suggest a school might be drifting from its mission. Like the proverbial "frog in the kettle," mission drift usually does not happen quickly or dramatically but gradually and over time, with changes that often seem unremarkable in and of themselves. Some of these changes are driven by cultural pressures, such as the demands that governments and businesses place on schools to change their views on marriage and sexuality, for one example. Other changes are made as a result of financial pressures, not uncommon among Christian colleges, most of whom are largely tuition driven with little to no endowment funds to provide a financial backstop. The financial pressures that students and parents face factor in here as well, putting a strain on the school to minimize the cost and the time to degree completion for the student. Still other changes are motivated by a desire for increased academic recognition and credibility, particularly among their peers in R1 research universities. Institutions should not underestimate these cultural, financial, and academic headwinds into which they are "flying their plane."

One of the most significant reasons that mission fidelity requires constant vigilance is that, historically, once a college or university has started drifting from its mission, turning it around is very difficult to accomplish. As we mentioned in chapter 3, some of the earliest and most renowned schools such as Harvard, Yale, and Princeton departed from their founders' goals and are nothing resembling what their founders envisioned. There are dozens and dozens of schools that have followed in their wake over the history of higher education in the United States.[1] Many of these schools were started by different denominations, and the drift of their sponsored colleges reflected the theological departure from orthodoxy of that particular denomination.

Whether or not a particular movement is indicative of mission drift depends on numerous factors, such as the stated mission of the

---

[1] See for examples, James Tunstead Burtchaell, *The Dying of the Light: The Disengagement of Christian Colleges and Universities from Their Christian Churches* (Grand Rapids: Eerdmans, 1998); George M. Marsden, *The Soul of the American University, Revisited: From Protestant to Postsecular*, 2nd ed. (New York: Oxford University Press, 2021). The first edition has a different subtitle, reflecting a bit different emphasis—*The Soul of the American University: From Protestant Establishment to Established Nonbelief* (New York: Oxford University Press, 1993).

school itself and many of the factors that determine the specific DNA of the school, as mentioned in chapter 3. We would suggest viewing potential signs of mission drift along a spectrum—some changes are *definitely not* signs of drift, some are *possibly* indications of drift, and some are *certainly* markers of departure from the original mission. Of course, not all departures from the founders' vision are necessarily problematic. Take, for example, schools that were founded with a racist past or founders who held racist views of African Americans. It is understandable that at some point in the school's history, the leadership would actively disassociate the school from that part of its past.

Perhaps the place to begin a more specific discussion of mission drift is with questions to be asked regularly. These are things that leaders should keep an eye on. There are rarely simple answers to these questions, but asking them helps to keep mission in the forefront of our minds.

1. What would our founders think of this specific change we are making?
2. More generally, what would our founders think if they came back to visit the campus today?
3. Whom are we inviting to campus in order for the university to advocate for and support their views? (Some speakers could be invited to the campus for the purpose of providing a first-hand look at and critical interaction with views with which we disagree—that is different from an invitation that supports and advocates the person's views.)
4. Whom are we honoring/celebrating in our public events and public communications? Are we honoring people who hold dear the things that we as an institution hold dear?
5. Which programs are being given funding priority?
6. What are our faculty publishing? Are they publishing material that is consistent with our theological convictions?

Other specific questions can begin to give an idea of where we are on a spectrum of mission drift. It helps leadership consider particular issues or controversies and discern whether they are "definitely not," "possibly," or "certainly" experiencing mission drift. An example of *definitely not* mission drift would be efforts to recruit and retain minority students in order to diversify the student body of the school. However, an office of DEI (diversity, equity, and inclusion) could possibly suggest mission drift if it introduces an ideology that is not consistent with Scripture. But with a strong theological foundation for diversity, such an office might not suggest drift but strengthen the school.

On the other side of the spectrum, an example of something that would *certainly* indicate mission drift would be changes to the published and public theological convictions of the school, especially if those changes touched some of the central doctrines of the Christian faith, such as the authority of the Bible, the deity of Christ, salvation by grace through faith, Christ's bodily resurrection, and his return. We would also suggest that a loosening of views on marriage and sexuality would constitute mission drift. Further examples of things that are certainly indicators of drift include loosening of vetting of faculty for missional and theological fit, faculty who are publishing positions that are directly at variance with the university's theological convictions, and a weakening of integration in the curriculum.

Examples of changes that are *possibly* indications of mission drift are things like a change in admission policies to admit non-Christian students. In the case of schools where the mission is more broadly evangelistic, it might very well be consistent with their founding mission to admit increasing numbers of non-Christian students. However, if done mainly for financial reasons, simply to attract more students regardless of their spiritual journey, it could be a sign of mission drift. Further examples of what is *possibly* mission drift include reductions to the Bible and theology curriculum, de-emphasis on the spiritual formation of students, and de-emphasis on chapel and other cocurricular elements of the student spiritual experience. Of course, these are not intended to be exhaustive but to be examples. We would strongly encourage each college or university to formulate their own set of indicators of mission drift given their founding, context, and organizational DNA.

Ensuring Missional and Theological Fit

Very few aspects of university life are more important to mission faithfulness than the hiring of faculty (both full-time and adjunct faculty) and cocurricular staff. The vetting and hiring process includes much more than simply the prospective faculty's academic qualifications and teaching ability—it also includes their theological and missional fit with the school. We would suggest that the cocurricular staff—those involved in student life and residential life, athletics coaches, chapel staff, and spiritual life staff—undergo an equally rigorous vetting for missional and theological fit as the full-time faculty (not to mention the senior leadership and board of trustees). In our view, the cocurricular side of the university is as influential in the lives of students as the classroom faculty, if not more so. The cocurricular staff are the ones who impact students at their crisis moments, most of which occur outside of regular classroom times, and they walk with them through college life in ways that the faculty are generally not able to. The impact of the cocurricular staff often goes under-noticed and underappreciated and can be highly formative for students in their spiritual and emotional lives. Conversely, we would suggest that the influence of cocurricular staff can be quite destructive to students if they do not hold dear the same commitments that the school does.

It is critical that *everyone involved in hiring recognize that mission fidelity is everyone's business.* From academic leaders to department chairs to those involved in search processes for potential faculty and cocurricular staff, ensuring mission fit cannot be relegated or delegated. The rigor and specific ways in which schools vet these roles for mission fit vary widely across the Christian college spectrum. We would strongly suggest that there is more to faculty hiring than what would be customary in a secular university—academic qualifications, prospects for research, and teaching ability (though teaching is sometimes not a major concern in R1 research universities). We would also suggest that the more rigorous the vetting for missional fit, the better. Of course, academic background, research trajectory, and teaching competence are critical components of a potential faculty member's qualifications. Those are necessary qualifications but not sufficient ones. Other qualifications include the inclination to invest in students' lives, the desire and aptitude to be involved in meaningful theological integration with his or her field, spiritual vitality and growth, church involvement, character and trustworthiness, and the state of his or her marriage and family, if applicable. For example, when I (Scott) interviewed for hiring at Biola University, one of the last interviews was with the president of the university, and my wife was also invited. The first question had to do with teaching—he asked, "How will your students know that you love them?" The second was directed to my wife—he asked, "How would you describe your husband's spiritual life?" To say that that question made me squirm in my seat a bit would be an understatement! But the president was getting at something he considered very important—that faculty care deeply for their students and that they have a vibrant spiritual life.

Vetting of faculty and cocurricular staff for missional fit also includes their adherence to the core convictions of the university. Missional fit is more than simple doctrinal adherence, but it is certainly not less than that. One way to get beyond merely signing off on a document is to ask candidates how they *feel* about these theological convictions. We do not mean feeling in a thin emotional sense, but rather in the sense of heartfelt regard. We should remember that a large part of our discipleship is the reordering and right-ordering of our loves—something that is at least partially revealed by asking "feeling" types of questions. We recognize that not all the school's doctrinal core will resonate equally deeply with every faculty candidate. But ensuring missional fit involves hiring faculty who not only affirm the doctrinal core of the school but who are also proud to be affiliated with a place that has your school's particular convictions and who love the things for which your school stands. Here are some questions that should be foremost in the minds of the people who are interviewing prospective faculty, and hopefully these questions can help guide specific questions that might be asked to candidates:

1. Do they hold dear what your school holds dear? (One might simply ask how candidates feel about the school's legacy. Is the school's legacy a treasured inheritance for them, or the starting point of a remodeling project that they would like to get underway?)

2. Do they wish that they were going to be at a secular university instead of a Christian one, but since they happened to be Christians, they are at least hoping they might get a job here? Do they actually have a vision and passion for a university grounded in a biblical worldview?

3. Do they treasure the opportunities your school provides for themselves and their students? If so, why do they treasure it?

4. Are there things about which they are excited at the prospect of doing at a Christian college/university that they would be unable to do at a secular university? If so, what are they, and why does the candidate find them so attractive?

There are several approaches a school can take to the process of ascertaining the theological fit of faculty and cocurricular staff. They can simply check the boxes and sign off on the theological commitments of the school. To be a bit more rigorous, they can be asked to articulate in writing their understanding of the particular doctrinal items specified by the school and reply in writing to queries from a designated reviewer (if the system includes such a person) and/or the dean. In our view, having an independent theological reviewer can be beneficial, since the reviewer is trained theologically and able to make the distinctions needed and tease out a candidate's views. In addition, we regularly bring in specific expertise in many other areas of the university, and it makes sense to bring in someone trained theologically to assist with a theological review, especially since the theological background of the dean could vary widely depending on his or her field. Further, the reviewer has no "skin in the game" with any candidate and avoids a conflict of interest that the dean might have. Additional rigor would be involved in requiring a doctrinal interview in which the candidates verbally articulate their views and have more of a conversation with the reviewer and dean. It may be that different levels of rigor are used for adjunct faculty than for full-time professors. For example, it may be that an actual interview is required for full-time faculty, whereas a written articulation, with an opportunity for clarifying questions, is sufficient for adjunct faculty candidates. When actual interviews are done, it is important that the dean and a theological reviewer (if separate from the dean, which we suggest it should be) sit on the same side of the table, both literally and figuratively, from the candidate. The reviewer should be there at the invitation of the dean, and the questions to be posed agreed upon in advance. However, if the reviewer feels the need to pursue a particular doctrinal area further, he or she should be able to pursue the necessary clarity of the candidate's views. The dean or hiring department chair should not view this part of the vetting process as something simply "to get the candidate through," nor should they coach candidates on how to answer questions that are raised. Nor should the hiring department view this process as something they can delegate to the theological side of the university, with the hiring department's role being simply to evaluate the candidate's academic and teaching qualifications. Remember, determining missional and theological fit is everyone's business.

A good way to think about the sort of vetting we are describing is that we want our candidates to tell stories about how they see their doctrinal beliefs playing out in practice. Agreeing with propositional affirmations of doctrinal beliefs is essential, but it is not sufficient for determining missional fit. Narrating one's beliefs, either by telling actual stories about how one has seen his or her doctrinal beliefs playing out in real-life situations, or describing how he or she would respond to real-life situations that have come up for other faculty on campus, or even by describing how he or she would respond to a hypothetical situation are all excellent approaches to understanding how a candidate would operationalize his or her faith and embody the Christian mission of the school.

Doing this sort of vetting requires more time than we often want to give. It is more of a long conversation than merely a series of questions and answers. This conversation could take place either remotely or, preferably, in person. It is important to remember that we are not asking candidates to be professional theologians but to be able to articulate their understanding of the school's core theological convictions and be able to address why they think they are true and how they matter in real life. In our view, being able to answer many of these questions is something we would expect not only from potential faculty but also from cocurricular staff, all of whom will be shaping students, not only academically but spiritually as well.

We will offer some specific examples of questions we use in interviews. They are used to start or deepen a conversation. They are not meant be a series of "gotcha" questions. These are questions that generally do not have simple right or wrong answers, but they can reveal the way a person thinks about his or her faith and how it contributes to his or her moral, personal, and spiritual reasoning. This is also a list of options, not a required list that is meant to be asked of every candidate in his or her interview. It is wise for anyone on the search team to ask these types of questions or similar follow-up questions. And finally, these questions should be tailored to the particular commitments most relevant to your school:

1. Suppose a student asks you, "Why do you believe in the resurrection of Jesus?," what would you tell him or her? (A follow-up question might be, "What would you say to a student who said that he or she believed in the resurrection but did not really know why it mattered?")

2. If a student said to you, "I think Jesus was a great moral teacher, but I am not so sure about Jesus being God," what would you say in response?

3. If a student asked you, "Why should I believe the Bible is a reliable account of the life of Jesus and early Christian history?" what would you tell him or her?

4. What does it mean to say that "Christ died for our sins?" (Or, one might ask, "How would you respond to a student who said, 'I am here because my mom and dad wanted me to go to a Christian school, but as I talk to people here, I think *Christian* means something different to me that it does to them. I am just wondering if you could help me understand what it means to be a Christian'?")

5. How would you respond to a Jewish or Muslim person who accuses you of worshipping three gods because you believe in the Trinity?

6. How would you respond to your astonished neighbor who says, "Surely you do not believe in angels and demons"?

7. What would you say to the student who is aghast at the idea of "God sending people to hell"?

8. What is the definition of the gospel?

9. How would you lead someone to faith in Christ? Possibly role-play this and see if the person can lead you to Christ.

10. What would you say to the student who insists that "I can have a vibrant spiritual life, but I do not need the church"?

11. How would you respond to a student who states that he lives out the gospel in actions only and is not comfortable trying to convert someone to Jesus?

12. How do you understand the relationship between social justice and the gospel?

13. What is your understanding of the morality of abortion and euthanasia?

14. What is your understanding of the point at which human personhood begins?

15. A student comes to you who has become pregnant, and she is wanting to seek an abortion since she is unmarried and unable to provide for a child. What would you say to her?

16. How do you understand the biblical mandate for creation care? How does climate change fit into creation care?

17. What is your view of the definition of marriage?

18. What would you say to a student who says, "Why can marriage not simply be any committed couple who loves each other, is committed to God, and wants to be monogamous?"

19. Do you believe God made people gay or lesbian, or is this a result of human brokenness and fallenness?

20. What would you say to a student who does not think a biblical view of marriage is worth dividing over because it is not a "gospel issue"?

21. Do you believe gender differences were part of God's design? In other words, are the differences between men and women part of divine design, the product of human fallenness, or mere social constructs?

22. Suppose a student came into your office and shared with you that she feels like she is a man trapped in a woman's body and

is considering cross-dressing and gender transition treatments. What would you say to this student?

23. How would you respond to a student who asks, "What is wrong with a person choosing a gender that best fits his or her experience?"

Creating a Culture Conducive to Integration

In chapter 4 it was suggested that the task of theological integration with the various academic disciplines is a hallmark of Christian colleges and universities. But although it is commonly aspired to, it is not easy to do. As we pointed out, most faculty who have been trained at secular universities receive virtually nothing in their training about how to think Christianly about their disciplines. As a result, they routinely come to our institutions as new faculty with a desire to think integratively about their fields, but without much aptitude or experience in doing so. At times, new faculty come to our school without even the inclination for integration, but rather with a sense that their first allegiance is to their academic guilds, and secondarily to the institution at which they are teaching. Potential faculty that have little to no interest in integration are a poor fit for those schools that are serious about integration. Creating a culture conducive to doing integration well is critical to fulfilling the mission of the university and to its integrity. Institutional integrity is compromised if the school advertises itself as Christian but does not regularly reflect this in the classroom. It sets students up for a potentially disappointing and disillusioning experience. *Whether or not an institution will actually offer a Christian higher education is largely dependent upon whether or not the faculty understand their disciplines from a distinctly Christian perspective.* Simply having scholars who happen to be Christians is not enough to ensure this. Rather, one needs to develop scholars with a profoundly Christian imagination for their disciplines. Here are some questions that can be used to help discern the interest a prospective faculty member has for doing integrative thinking:

1. How do you understand the concept of the integration of Christian faith and your discipline?
2. What do you see as the highest priorities for a scholar working under the lordship of Christ in your particular academic field?
3. How does your approach to your particular discipline help students capture a vision that the Christian worldview is true and good?
4. How does your approach to your discipline in your teaching and writing cause students (readers) to grow in the confidence that Christianity (as understood by historic Christianity) is true and rational?
5. What things in your discipline seem to be reasonable and support a Christian worldview? How do you showcase these to your students?
6. What specific presuppositions, methodologies, or trends in your field of study, if any, do you find to be *consistent* with the Bible and a historic Christian worldview?
7. What specific worldview presuppositions, methodologies, or trends in your field of study, if any, do you find to be *inconsistent* with the Bible and a historic Christian worldview? How would you showcase these differences to your students?
8. How will your students see you and your discipline as distinctly and robustly Christian in both your life and teaching?

Resourcing Faculty Members for Integration

Integration of faith and learning does not happen automatically or accidentally. Particularly in a contemporary academic culture that either ignores or is actively antagonistic to the gospel, one cannot expect that faculty will acquire a vibrant theological imagination for their academic disciplines from their graduate programs. Nor is it common for contemporary preaching in local churches to be robust enough to equip scholars for substantive Christian engagement with their chosen fields. Our faculty desperately need models and mentors who integrate the historic Christian faith with the best of human learning. They need collegial discussions that foster thinking that is both creative and faithful. They need to become acquainted with the rich and diverse intellectual resources within the Christian tradition—resources that touch on every facet of creation and culture. In short, if we expect to fulfill the mission of Christian higher education, Christian universities need to provide institutional support for training and equipping our faculty to think Christianly about their disciplines.

Worked examples are helpful, so we will give some short descriptions of what we have done at Biola to help resource our faculty. We offer no systematic study that demonstrates these to be the best activities one might do, nor can we assure that these are sufficient for equipping faculty. In fact, we have learned there is always more to do. These are just activities that have been successful enough that we keep doing them; it is a list of our best efforts. It should be noted that no faculty member is expected to participate in all these activities. We try to keep required trainings to a minimum and draw in a large portion of our faculty simply by providing things that they are genuinely interested in doing. It should be noted that we have a three-quarter time faculty position and a full-time assistant director who oversee this work. Your institution may not have the resources to do all these things or the staff to manage them, but many of these activities can be (and have been) done with very little cost to the institution. The most important thing is to start where you are and add bits and pieces to your resourcing as you go along.

Coalition of the Willing (year-long small group cohort)

The Coalition of the Willing is a collegial, spiritual, and academic experience that over 140 faculty members have completed in the past fifteen years. It is a year-long small-group experience with six to eight other faculty members that focuses on the integration of faith and learning. It normally meets about six or seven times each semester for discussions of specific content related to theology and the integration of faith and learning (usually over a meal). In addition, it includes a spiritual formation retreat at a nearby retreat center. During the second semester, we look at theological issues as we find them embedded in our life and culture. This is done through a series of "experiential" components determined by the interests and expertise of our group. Past experiences have included trips to art museums, an interview with a Hollywood screen writer, a visit to the Japanese American National Museum, a visit to the Holocaust Museum, reading and discussing a novel, visiting a laboratory, a visit to a mosque, and a host of other fascinating experiences.

We have also done departmental Coalitions of the Willing for individual academic departments to help them develop a vision of the integration of faith and learning that is "indigenous" to their academic discipline and also expresses the particular passions and concerns of the individuals who make up the department.

FIS (Faculty Integration Seminar)

The Faculty Integration Seminar (FIS) brings a leading theologian or biblical scholar to campus from outside the university for a week-long residency with approximately fifteen of our faculty. The faculty participants are selected from a pool of applicants approximately six months before the residency. They are given an extensive reading list in preparation for the seminar. At the end of this time, the faculty are required to write a fifteen-page paper integrating theological concepts and their academic discipline.

This event has taken place annually (with some years excepted) since 1994 and is the longest running training program that we do. Since the faculty are paid a stipend for attending the seminar in lieu of being able to teach a summer school class, this seminar is easily the most expensive training experience we offer. It is also the most demanding event we do in terms of time and requirements. Nonetheless, it has also been extremely well received and has proven particularly valuable not only because of the in-depth learning and discussion but also because it has fostered many collegial, cross-disciplinary projects among our faculty.

Foundations Roundtable

The Foundations Roundtable is intended to promote understanding and appreciation of the theological commitments and distinctives of Biola University. We offer this in part to prepare and equip faculty to think through the doctrinal statement for tenure and promotion. It also serves as a means of helping faculty understand the significance of doctrine for the integration of faith and learning and also for addressing important issues within contemporary life and culture. Foundations Roundtable usually consists of a small cohort that meets about four or five times in a given semester. We do readings of theological material related to the theological distinctives or the articles of faith in preparation for our discussion.

Coaching conversations

These structured coaching conversations are done with individual faculty members over a semester or year. They take an in-depth look at one of the classes the faculty member is currently teaching and follow an intentional coaching process to help faculty develop an integration experience for their students that is theologically robust but also deepens their students' understanding of their academic discipline.

The coaching conversations usually involve six or more ninety-minute meetings spread over the course of the semester (or year). The conversations begin with a general discussion of the class content, the opportunities for integration, and the integrative assignments within the current course syllabus/content. The remaining conversations explore options for deepening the learning experiences both theologically and experientially, with the end result being an integrative experience that is developed and implemented by the faculty member, is embedded seamlessly into the essential content of the class, and is much more satisfying for both the students and the faculty member than the current assignments are. Since these coaching experiences could be done by Zoom, they were first implemented during COVID lockdowns as an alternative to other training opportunities that we provided. We soon discovered, however, that the coaching times were very effective from a missional standpoint, so we have continued to offer them.

Faculty reading groups

One of the most valuable and flexible training resources we have sponsored is faculty reading groups. These groups usually meet three to four times a semester to discuss a book or a set of articles. Faculty from a wide range of disciplines participate. We have read and discussed academic treatises (for example, *A Secular Age* by Charles Taylor, *Faith, Love and Poetry* by Malcolm Guite), articles on a particular theme (art and theology, secularism, embodiment and incarnation, creation care), and novels (*Zero K: A Novel* by Don DeLillo, *The Road* by Cormac McCarthy, *Jayber Crow* by Wendell Berry). Box lunches are usually provided for the group members, as well as purchasing the books. The goal of these groups is to cultivate the ability to see important theological themes as they come to us embedded in both academic research and literary works.

Image reading groups

Many years ago, a new faculty member was hired to teach photo-journalism. He was very experienced in his profession, deeply committed in his faith, but largely unfamiliar with integrating faith and learning. He was eager to learn, so I (Rick) invited him to bring along a half-dozen of his favorite photographs to my office and we would talk about them. We spent an hour or two just "reading" these images. We talked about what we saw in the photographs, how and why they moved us, and the glimpses they gave of the plight of human life, as well as the glimmers of hope they offered. It was such an enjoyable time that we kept doing it all semester. The following year we pioneered an "image reading group" based on this experience. It was facilitated by one of our art professors and targeted toward faculty from the School of Fine Arts and Communication. In following semesters, faculty from across campus have joined in. Together they view and discuss images—photographs, paintings, scenes from movies, and the like. These groups have had a wide variety of benefits, helping participants to attend more carefully to the world around them, to see the traces of theology that are always embedded in cultural artifacts, and simply to enjoy deep and thought-provoking conversations inspired by the images set before us and before which we set ourselves.

Table Talk

Table Talk is a lunchtime colloquium usually led by one or two of our own faculty, though we have often used outside speakers as well. The goal of our Table Talks is modeling integration of faith and learning as well as offering teaching that addresses important issues from a distinctively Christian perspective. We usually organize the content for each semester around a particular theme. Past themes have included politics, human sexuality, visions of human flourishing, visual arts, positive psychology and virtue, and other important contemporary issues. We usually film these presentations and post them on our website. The events are done over lunch, providing an opportunity to connect with fellow faculty members.

New faculty integration training workshop

After our new faculty members have completed their first year of teaching, they are required to participate in a three-day integration training workshop. This workshop is geared for classroom teaching, and we intentionally schedule it after our new faculty have had some hands-on experience teaching their classes. Our hope is that faculty members who complete this workshop will:

1. Have a deeper understanding of core doctrines of the Christian faith that pertain to creation and culture.
2. Understand what the integration of faith and learning means in practical terms within their academic disciplines.
3. Be equipped with models for integrating faith and learning that are interesting and compelling.
4. Have prepared at least one in-depth example of integrating faith and learning within their own classroom settings.

The workshop offers general teaching regarding the integration of faith and learning, hands-on engagement with examples of good integrative classroom experiences, and small-group discussions. On the final day, each faculty member has a chance to workshop an integrative classroom experience with his or her colleagues and receive feedback and encouragement. A very similar workshop had been done for adjunct faculty—specifically targeting those who teach regularly in our programs.

Co-teaching teams for BBST 465 seminars

Each of our undergraduate students is required to take an "integration seminar," which is a capstone class that draws on the material the students have learned in their Bible and theology classes and applies it to either the student's academic major or else to an important issue related to contemporary culture. We have done integration seminars for a wide variety of academic majors including Journalism, Communications, Music & Worship, Art, Psychology, Business, Cinema & Media Arts, Education, English, History, Nursing, and more. Integration seminars for contemporary issues have included seminars on Money, Sex, and Power; on Work and Calling; on The Bible and the Good Society; on Identity and the Incarnation; and many more. These seminars model integration for our students, but more importantly they contribute to the spiritual formation of our students by helping them think through the implications of Christian theology for the challenges of daily life.

We have worked very hard to make these seminars team taught, particularly when they are associated with a particular major. The teams combine a faculty member from the academic disciplines with a theologian or biblical scholar, allowing the faculty to model integrative conversations directly in the classroom, and also providing a great ongoing training experience that sharpens the integrative skills of our faculty.

One of the institutional challenges of doing co-taught seminars is the cost. The classes are relatively small (usually capped at twenty-five students), and this makes having two professors in the classroom very expensive if the class counts toward each professor's teaching load. The work-around we devised to lessen the cost of co-teaching was to identify one faculty member as the "faculty of record" and the other faculty member as the "stipended" faculty. Both faculty members are in the classroom for most or all the class sessions. However, the person who is the faculty of record is responsible for grading and managing class-related tasks. The stipended faculty member plays a role that is analogous to a guest lecturer except they are there every week. For most faculty, that means they are doing all of what they enjoy most about teaching and none of the things they enjoy least. They are paid approximately two-thirds of what they would be paid to teach an overload class. This system has worked well, though there are predictable challenges that arise from sabbaticals, changes in departmental teaching assignments, and the variable availability of faculty for doing overload classes.

Web-based resources

Over the course of years, we have developed a series of web-based training videos that we call "iFLIPs" (an acronym for Internet Faith Learning Integration Presentations). These iFLIPs give a basic overview of the integration of faith and learning and some practical ideas for classroom instruction and student projects. We make these resources available on the theologylived.com website. Though we originally developed these for training faculty, we have found they are very useful to students as well. They are frequently used in classes—both online and on campus. The iFLIPs have also been translated into Russian, Ukrainian, and subtitled in Mandarin for use in international settings. In addition to the iFLIPs, we also use the theologylived.com website as an archive for Table Talks and other special colloquia that are related to the integration of faith and learning.

Conclusion

Culture matters. Institutional culture matters to the mission of Christian higher education. Academic and cocurricular leaders are responsible for creating and sustaining the culture of the university so that integration is encouraged, expected, resourced, and rewarded. Mission faithfulness is not something that can be placed on "automatic pilot." It requires constant nurture and constant vigilance. It is subject to entropy, the natural movement from order to disorder, if left unattended for too long. It is quite possible today to have a Christian college or university that is financially strong, academically rigorous, and housed in state-of-the-art facilities. It can have a prestigious faculty and accomplished and influential graduates. But if it has lost its missional moorings, its leaders will have failed; the school will soon join dozens of others that have historically succumbed to mission drift. May it not be so for your institution.

Questions

1. What is the process that your institution uses to vet faculty for doctrinal and missional fit? Do you believe it is adequate to safeguard the school's mission? Do you have any suggestions to improve the rigor of your process?
2. Does your institution use a similar process for vetting cocurricular staff for mission fit? Why or why not?
3. What would be some of the signs of mission drift that would be specific to your school?
4. What questions would you add to ours to help get a better sense of a potential faculty member's theological and missional commitments?

CHAPTER 6

WHAT IS THE CHRISTIAN GRADUATE?

Universities must articulate their educational vision
as a description of persons, not just programs.

In my (Rick's) job as the Director of the Office of Faith and Learning, I frequently have visiting leaders from other Christian colleges sent my way to talk about integration of faith and learning. I have learned a lot through these conversations over the years—including many things that have helped us build our own program. But I have also had some disconcerting conversations. One conversation I recall was with a senior administrator from a small Christian school who wanted some input on training and equipping faculty. We talked about the importance of getting faculty aligned with the school's Christian mission, but her description of the school's mission centered on various events and activities related to community service and social justice. I asked if there was anything distinctively Christian about the school's vision for social justice or about the way they worked to achieve it. Her answers made it clear that there was not. I asked if and how they saw the educational experience at their college deepening the faith of their graduates. She said, "That's not the way we normally talk about it. We use the word *Christian* to talk about the institution as a whole. We don't really talk a lot about the Christian faith of the students."

I realized in that moment that I had stumbled upon an important distinction. There is a world of difference between using the word *Christian* to describe *institutions* and using the word *Christian* to describe *persons*. For example, this book has talked a lot about the telos or purpose of Christian higher education. One might ask if we have been thinking about persons who help make Christian institutions, or institutions who help make Christian persons. If anyone is wondering, we mean the latter. Our concern is for the kind of *persons* our educational institutions form. Institutions are important—but decisions about structuring our institutions should be guided by the kinds of graduates we hope to produce. This chapter will offer some reflections on what a Christian higher education contributes to the formation of the Christian faith of their graduates.

One could view this chapter as an attempt to answer Peter Drucker's fourth question: "What are our results?" At any university, *the graduates are the results*; at Christian universities, our results are Christian graduates. The genius of Drucker's questions is that they require us to make explicit what we often take for granted. For example, it is easy to say that we want our "results" to be graduates who are faithful Christians in heart and mind, but what would that really look like? So we will sketch a vision of what faithfulness looks like in both heart and mind. Then we will move on to an example drawn from our own experience that teases out ways that this can help guide curricular and cocurricular decisions. In so doing, we will move from answering Drucker's fourth question (what are our results?) to the beginnings of answering Drucker's fifth question (what is our plan?). The point of this discussion is to help institutional leadership to become explicit about the kinds of students they want to graduate. Once this is clear, one can evaluate current programs and plans with a critical eye to see (1) if they actually correspond with the institution's vision for its graduates, and (2) whether or not they are effective.

"What Do You Want to Be When You Grow Up?"

William Willimon and Thomas Naylor served on the faculty of Duke University and co-taught a class entitled "The Search for Meaning." Their experience teaching this class, combined with some research they did on the perceived purpose of higher education, led them to believe that there was a crisis in higher education, not only at Duke but at North American universities in general. One example they relate is particularly instructive:

> For several years, students in our School of Business were asked to write a personal strategic plan for the ten-year period after their graduation. The question posed to them was, "What do you want to be when you grow up?" With few exceptions, they wanted three things: money, power, and things (very big things, including vacation homes, expensive foreign automobiles, yachts, and even airplanes). Primarily concerned with their careers and the growth of their financial portfolios, their personal plans contained little room for family, intellectual development, spiritual growth, or social responsibility.
>
> Their mandate to the faculty was, "Teach me how to be a money-making machine." "Give me only the facts, tools, and techniques required to ensure my instantaneous financial success." All else was irrelevant.[1]

---

[1] William H. Willimon and Thomas H. Naylor, *The Abandoned Generation: Rethinking Higher Education* (Grand Rapids: Eerdmans, 1995), 38–39.

These elite students were being asked a question about the telos of their education. They had come to business school for a reason. The question was intended to make that reason clear to themselves as well as their faculty. Their answers were instructive. Their vision for their "grown-up" life was money, power, and things. Willimon and Naylor wondered whether this was actually what Duke intended for the graduates of their business school.

The point of this story is not to shame a particular set of graduate students for being greedy but rather to point out the value of asking a question like, "What do we want our graduates to be when they grow up?" It is a good question for every educational institution to ask itself, not just its students. It would be good for incoming students and the university to agree upon what they believe the educational project to be about. What are the hallmarks of a well-formed graduate? How would an institution identify a graduate who was successfully shaped and formed by their four years (or more) of higher education? Willimon and Naylor describe a set of business school students who, if given what they wanted, would be dismally greedy and painfully self-absorbed. These are not qualities most universities would want to see in their graduates, but what would one want to find in one's graduates instead? The university must articulate their educational vision as a description of *persons*, not just programs.

Returning to the five different cultures of a university discussed in chapter 1, one could easily see differences in the way these cultures might be expressed in terms of a vision for a graduate. Here is a set of descriptions of graduates that reflect these different cultures (slightly paraphrased from statements found on university websites):

Higher education for the sake of a job: We seek to graduate students with a clear vision for their desired careers, and *the essential credentials, hands-on-skills, and network of fellow graduates* required to get them jobs within their chosen fields.

Higher education for the sake of social activism: We seek to graduate students who are *socially responsible practitioners*, employing knowledge, empathy, compassion, and courage *to drive action and create real change in the social inequities within local institutional structures and throughout the world.*

Higher education for the sake of a truth: We seek to graduate students who *contribute to the advancement of humankind through the rigorous and relentless pursuit of knowledge.*

Higher education for the sake of self-actualization: We seek to graduate students prepared to thrive as independent, innovative leaders *within their chosen life paths.*

Higher education for the sake of human flourishing: We seek to graduate students who know how to discern the truth and distinguish it from error, are acquainted with the broad scope of human learning, and are *equipped to live a truly free and human life.*

These statements are drawn from various secular schools, so it is natural to consider what might be different if one were describing a Christian graduate. A cursory examination of websites of Christian colleges and universities found statements such as these (again, loosely paraphrased):

- We seek to graduate students who are prepared for a career, but also *shaped into thoughtful, service-minded, and engaged members of their community and world.*
- We seek to graduate students to the highest standards of academic excellence and Christian values, *who are strengthened for lives of purpose, service, and leadership.*
- We seek to graduate *thoughtful scholars, grateful servants, and faithful leaders for global engagement with the academy, church, and world.*

- We seek to graduate students who engage the culture and change the world *by being people of competence and character, becoming people of wisdom, and modeling grace-filled community.*

These statements come from vision or mission statements of Christian colleges and universities. Statements like this are usually written to be more inspirational than informational. They are never meant to offer a strategic plan. Therefore, it is unsurprising that they lack details necessary for actually guiding institutional decision-making. But if one looks closely, one will realize that they lack something more than just specificity. What is notable by its absence is content that is *distinctively Christian.* The qualities that are given could equally well be found in graduates of a secular institution since they too seek to graduate students who, for example, live lives *of purpose, service, and leadership.* Unique qualities of a *Christian* graduate remain unspecified. Further probing of the websites of many Christian colleges, one would find language that describes Christian aspects of the *institution* (that it has a Christian history, Christian legacy, or Christian values) but much less about the faith and practice they hope to see in the lives of the graduates themselves. In some cases, this is likely due to open enrollment policies, which means that their student body includes those who are not believers. But even in such cases, one would hope there is a clear vision of what the institution hopes to contribute to the formation of their *Christian* students.

A Christian university should have a clear vision of how their education seeks to form genuine and committed disciples of Christ. This need not be described in a vision statement, but it must be articulated somewhere and not just assumed or described in a dusty volume housed in a neglected institutional archive. It must be articulated clearly, actively, and in ways that help operationalize it into institutional life. Such a description is not a marketing tool, though the marks of a successful graduate could certainly be used in recruiting prospective students. It is much more vital, however, that the vision of a successful graduate shape every aspect of the university, including curricular decisions, the structure of general education, the way community is formed in residence halls, the offerings of cocurricular facets of the university, the choice of board members, the choice of chapel and graduation speakers, stories in university magazines, and every other facet of the university. For this to happen, much more detailed thinking must be done.

Marks of a Christian Graduate

As was stated at the beginning of this book, for Christian higher education to be successful, it must succeed at both being Christian and being higher education. Therefore, we will identify qualities of a distinctively Christian *mind* and of a thriving Christian *faith*. We will also attempt to unpack these at a level specific enough to guide institutional decision-making. These descriptions might find their way into value statements, planning documents, or evaluations and assessments. The point is to implement them in places where decisions are actually made.

The mind of the Christian graduate

The Christian mind is in no way exempt from embracing educational rigors and acquiring the skills necessary for academic endeavors of the highest level. All the normal demands for structuring, implementing, and assessing education apply equally to sacred and secular education. However, it is worth noting some unique qualities found in the Christian educational context.

Unity of learning

In the modern era, universities and medicine have followed parallel tracks of ever-increasing specialization. Dramatic advances in knowledge and technology have resulted. In both cases, however, the whole has been neglected for the sake of the parts. In the case of medicine, the discipline of family practice has become its own medical specialization defined by its concern with the *total health care of the individual and the family*, as opposed to focusing on a particular organ system or disease. Likewise in higher education, disciplines like art, literature, history, social science, political science, and psychology all study what it means to be human through different lenses. What is often lacking, however, is faculty dedicated to bringing all these lenses into a single field of vision. Interdisciplinary classes are an attempt to do this, though it is often done in a piecemeal fashion with little continuity or commitment.

The Christian faith, however, can offer a point of contact that unites the university. For Christians, the arts and humanities as well as sciences and professional studies are viewed as a gift from God intended to help us fulfill the creation mandate—our call to multiply, fill, rule, and subdue the world. All of creation and all of humanity are the product of divine craftsmanship. And like any other craftsman, God has intentions and purposes for what he makes. The created order is *ordered*. It is not to be exploited for our own purposes but rather stewarded according to divine purposes. So what unites all spheres of human learning (and hence all academic disciplines) is a single vocation to see Christ enthroned as Lord in every aspect of the created order and every sphere of human endeavor. The development and use of every new technology, the advance of every frontier of knowledge—all come together in the task of glorifying Christ.

Community of learning

There are also resources that are uniquely available to Christians and that contribute to educational excellence. Norman Klassen and Jens Zimmermann point out that for a Christian . . . the church—that bastion of authority and dogma—can play a decisively enabling role in intellectual formation. For the intellectual pilgrim, the church provides a picture that is coherent but not complete. As the individual acquires new ideas and outlooks, she or he can try them on in the context of a specific community of a kind that is not readily available elsewhere. . . . When we engage the church, we engage something much larger than ourselves. There is also a regularity to church life that makes it an ongoing dialogue partner, chafing and uncompromising though it may be. The church also represents a historic community, the thinking, practices, and memories of people who have coalesced around a cluster of sacred mysteries for thousands of years. The individual who interrogates the church with new questions and perspectives often finds that the questions are not always new, not always shocking. They have often been asked before. The individual, in her turn, is challenged by the church in ways a dilettante of the latest ism may never be held to account by any intellectual "community."[2]

Klassen and Zimmermann identify a profoundly valuable resource for excellent education—a multigenerational, multicultural, worldwide learning community that has sustained a conversation for almost two thousand years about matters that touch on almost every facet of human learning. This is a powerful resource for Christian education. It should not only be acknowledged, but it must also be owned and cultivated by the faculty in service of their students. This is challenging if faculty have not had any formal training in Christian history or theology. This does not mean Christian schools should only hire those

    [2] Norman Klassen and Jens Zimmermann, *The Passionate Intellect: Incarnational Humanism and the Future of University Education* (Grand Rapids: Baker Academic, 2006), 41–42.

who have graduated from Christian schools, but it does mean that each Christian school should have a good answer to the question of when and how their faculty will acquire a substantial knowledge of Christian thought regarding their disciplines. Even though many modern academic disciplines seem remote from Christian thought, they rest on a particular vision of human flourishing. They ask and answer questions about the goals of a human life; they rest on assumptions about truth and knowledge; they tell origin stories about the nature of reality; and they usually offer a particular vision of the good, the true, and the beautiful. All in all, there are almost always substantive and interesting discussions of Christian theology and history that overlap the concerns of an academic discipline.

A Christian learning community is not just about intellectual content but also about life within the classroom itself. This is not to say that the classroom should be conducted like a church service but rather that the classroom should practice what the Christian faith teaches. David I. Smith, a professor at Calvin College who has written extensively on Christian pedagogy, tells of the story of two different parent-teacher conferences attended at his child's Christian high school. In the first conference, the teacher walked through all the grades their son had gotten, noted that they were all good, and then stated it was a successful semester thus far. He and his wife walked a few feet down the hall to the next class and experienced a very different teacher with a very different vision for what goes on in a Christian classroom.

> He shook our hands, introduced himself, found out which student was ours, and then paused. After a few moments' reflection, he commented that there was another student, sitting in the row behind our child in class, who had some learning difficulties and often found it difficult during long science classes to keep

track of what was going on. He had noticed our child choosing tactful moments to turn around and make sure that this other learner knew what was happening. He particularly appreciated this, he said, because he had been emphasizing throughout the semester that the class should function as a Christian learning community, and that meant that there should be a shared focus on making sure that all were included and enabled to learn. He saw the moments of turning around to help another student as an important contribution to the class, and he let that valuation be known. He concluded with some further comments on the class, and invited our questions.[3]

In the second case, the teacher clearly understood that there was a lot of Christian learning that went on in a classroom beyond just the content that was presented. Students learn by being part of a particular kind of community. He stated that they were to be a Christian learning community; he had a specific idea of what that might be (in this case, loving and caring for one another within the classroom); he recognized when that was happening and celebrated that by describing it to parents as an important part of assessing the progress of their child as well as the progress of the learning community as a whole.

The faith of the Christian graduate

Christian education must build Christian minds, but it must also contribute to the formation of a Christian faith. What sort of a faith should a Christian college seek to instill in its graduates? Here are some suggestions:

---

[3] David I. Smith, *On Christian Teaching: Practicing Faith in the Classroom* (Grand Rapids: Eerdmans, 2018), 84.

Durable faith

Developing a durable faith that is able to stand the test of time and tri-als must be one of the most important concerns of parents, churches, and Christian schools alike. A recent Pew Research Center study found that each new generation sees 31 percent of people who were raised Christian become religiously unaffiliated by the time they reach thirty.[4] Such statistics oversimplify a complex issue like deconversion, but there is no doubt that this is a difficult time in which to raise young people who have a durable, lifelong faith. Paul exhorts Timothy to follow the pattern of teaching that he passed on to him and to guard that good deposit (1 Tim 6:20). This same exhortation must be taken up by every generation, and it is a fair expectation of a Christian college that it con-tribute to deepening, sustaining, and guarding the faith of its students.

Examined faith

It was Socrates who said that an unexamined life is not worth living. For Christians, the same concern might be expressed this way: "An unexamined faith is not faithful." Jesus commands us to love God with all our heart, soul, mind, and strength. Loving God with our mind is not optional. Our faith is more than just intellectual, and there is always a danger in over-intellectualizing one's faith, but there is no dodging the fact that part of faithful discipleship is developing a Christian mind. And if there is a facet of faithful discipleship that falls squarely on the shoulders of Christian higher education, it is the development of the Christian mind.

---

[4] Pew Research Center, "Modeling the Future of Religion in America," Pew Research, September 13, 2022, https://www.pewresearch.org/religion/2022/09/13/modeling-the-future-of-religion-in-america/.

Attached faith

In recent years there has been a notable trend of Christians distancing themselves from the church. This is partly due to scandals among Christian leaders and divisions within local church congregations, but the problem is both deeper and broader than that. Particularly in the case of contemporary American culture, there is a tendency to conceive of the Christian faith in very individualistic terms—as if following Christ is done in one's inner heart, as if we stand before the face of God in isolation from others. But the New Testament knows nothing of such an isolated faith. New Testament faith is a faith that is experienced, expressed, and nurtured in the context of a body of believers. The presence of Christ and the work of the Holy Spirit are manifest in the living body of Christ. If we disconnect from the body, we will ultimately grow cold and disconnected from Christ. Furthermore, we are also connected to believers throughout all of church history. The Christian faith is a rooted faith. We stand before God, but we also stand before a great cloud of witnesses. Disconnecting from local church bodies or disparaging the faithfulness of those who have gone before us diminishes our faith. In the contemporary academy, disparaging the historical church is a cottage industry—one that is often practiced within the Christian academy as well. We must have a faith robust enough to acknowledge the failings of our contemporaries and our forebears, acknowledging their failings as we do our own. At the same time, we must also cherish the faith that Christians in every age held in their earthen vessels, be inspired by their faithfulness, and be warned by their failings, all while diligently guarding the deposit of the gospel that they entrusted to us. Christian higher education is a stewardship of the legacy of all who have gone before. We must both sift and savor that legacy.

Active faith

We are saved by grace through faith, but genuine faith is manifest in action. This does not mean every Christian must be an activist, but it does mean we must be active. We live our faith out in the world even if this world is not our home. We love our neighbors, be they friends or enemies. We do good so that all people might give glory to our Father who is in heaven. If people persecute us instead, we do good to them nonetheless. Christian higher education is not content to produce intellects that turn in upon themselves or that begin and end their thought within the boundaries of an academic discipline. A well-formed Christian mind is one that sees the world itself and all we do within it as an occasion for glorifying Christ.

Informed faith

The sons of Issachar were known as people who "understood the times and knew what Israel should do" (1 Chr 12:32). Christian higher education seeks to form graduates with the wisdom to read their time and the courage to engage in the battles of their day. We cannot simply look backward and defend the ground that was held by previous generations. We embrace a faith that was once for all delivered to the saints, but it is also a faith that must be instantiated in every generation and in every culture to which it spreads. Christian higher education offers one of the very best places for deep under-standing of the culture—its hopes, fears, doubts, and aspirations. It can examine all these critically and draw from the vast resources of Scripture and the best of human learning to address the needs of our cultural moment. Sometimes that may mean directly answering questions that the culture is asking; sometimes that may mean asking better questions. At times we will soothe fears, and at other times we may point out that our culture is fearing the wrong things. At times we will be a voice of hope, and at other times we will speak a word of prophetic warning. The wisdom to discern the most necessary action at any time and place requires a deeply informed faith—but also a faith that is informed by the realities of the world without being conformed to its standards.

Valued faith

Paul frequently finds occasion to remind people not to be ashamed of the gospel. That is a word that speaks to all who are involved in higher education. Pressure from public perception, academic peers in secular institutions, the professional organizations that govern our guilds, and countless other cultural forces create enormous pressure for Christian academics. This makes it attractive to minimize one's Christian profile, to edit some activities out of one's CV, to be silent when awkward issues are raised, and to apologize for the conduct of the church, both past and present. These same forces will be felt by our students, especially as they move on to graduate programs and their professional careers. One of the best things we can do for our students is to model for them an unashamed faith that proclaims the gospel even as it acknowledges points of honest tension and Christian failures. In *The Chronicles of Narnia*, C. S. Lewis memorably describes Aslan, the Christ figure in the story, telling the children they are "sons of Adam and daughters of Eve. And that is both honour enough to erect the head of the poorest beggar, and shame enough to bow the shoulders of the greatest emperor on earth."[5] The same could be said of the church—it has had its moments of both honor and shame. One cannot, with integrity, tell the story of the church as if it were a perfect tale of glowing deeds of faithfulness. However, we do need to be the curators of the real story of

---

[5] C. S. Lewis, *Prince Caspian: The Return to Narnia; Book 2 in The Chronicles of Narnia*, 1st Collier Books ed. (New York: Collier Books, 1970), 211–12.

the church, which entails seasons of both glory and darkness and often moments where both emerge together. And the story of the gospel needs to be told without shame, proclaimed in our scholarship as well as our conduct, for it remains the power of God unto salvation for all men and women, in any age and every place.

A Worked Example

There is much to be said about the qualities one might want to cultivate in the graduates of a Christian university. We will stop at that point, however, and shift our attention to an equally important question—how can a description like this aid in the planning and structuring of institutional life? To this end, we will briefly describe how this has worked in our own setting at Biola University. This is not because we have worked this out so well but rather because this is the setting we know the best and also because the challenges that Biola has faced are very similar to those faced by every other Christian school. It is our hope that describing some of the specific issues that have worked out in our context will stimulate thinking for specific issues faced by other schools.

In recent years we have confronted significant headwinds in higher education: increasing costs, decreasing enrollment, increasing regulation, expanding demands for data and assessment to justify curricular effectiveness, and conflicting recommendations from "experts," as well as conflicting demands from stakeholders. As a bonus, we navigated a global pandemic within the confines of Los Angeles County—which had one of the most restrictive COVID guidelines in the country. Pressures like these make for a certain amount of institutional soul-searching, and it is an unwritten law that universities search their souls by forming committees. We both served on our share. One of these committees was organized to look at the way in which we carry out

Christian formation. One tangible way Biola expresses its commitment to Christian formation is by requiring thirty units of Bible classes for virtually all our graduates. This is a big curricular commitment that is very specific to Biola—as far as we know, only one other CCCU school has such a large Bible requirement. But Christian formation is not limited to the classroom. We viewed a Biola education as the product of our community life, not just of our curriculum. Therefore, the committee included faculty, but also leaders of our cocurricular programs, administrative staff, alumni who were modeling qualities we wanted in our graduates, and some external individuals who were knowledgeable about Biola. This was an intentional effort to acknowledge that a lot of Christian formation happens outside the classroom. What we teach matters, but so does how we teach, how we live with one another in residence halls, how our athletic teams are coached and how they compete, and how our clubs are led and the sorts of activities they offer. All of these were clearly contributors to the Christian formation of our graduates.

We began by asking each member of the committee to contribute to a running list of characteristics we value in our graduates. Here is a short sample of the more than fifty items that were suggested:

- Graduates would draw their purpose, power, and direction from Christ through daily engagement with and devotion to Scripture.
- Graduates would be members in good standing of a local church and equipped whenever called to fill leadership positions.
- Graduates would be more and more aware of their sin than that of others—along with having an increasing confidence in God's grace in Christ and a corresponding humility and love.
- Graduates would not just be able to articulate the doctrine of union with Christ but would also habitually return to being

created, chosen, redeemed, justified, and glorified "in him" as the source of their personal identities.

- Graduates would know the Bible, especially its unfolding drama around Christ from Genesis to Revelation, and know how to practice sound hermeneutical rules for interpreting Scripture.
- Graduates would demonstrate the capacity to tolerate ambiguity, uncertainty, and mystery as it pertains to their faith.
- Graduates would be equipped to graciously engage with people who have varying political beliefs from a biblical perspective.
- Graduates would evidence a deep respect for the dignity of all people as well as diverse perspectives.
- Graduates would live out God's Word in the marketplace and be a light in the sometimes dark places where they may work.
- Graduates would be knowledgeable of the whole Bible, comfortable articulating its storyline, and deeply acquainted with core statements of their faith (e.g., the Nicene and Apostles' Creeds).
- Graduates would base their imitation of Christ on the historical person and work of Christ and not on cultural fads or personal assumptions about Jesus.

The running list was then refined, organized, and edited into a manageable number of outcomes. These were then arranged to correspond with our university's statement of values, which identifies truth (patterns of thought), transformation (patterns of heart), and testimony (patterns of action). Here is the list of Christian formation outcomes that we ended up with:

Truth Learning Scripture	Transformation Loving Scripture	Testimony Living Scripture
Biblically grounded Graduates know and interpret the Bible and are able to communicate its Christ-centered storyline and are familiar with the historic Christian faith.	*Identity in Christ* Graduates are confident in their identity in Christ, are humbly aware of their own sin, and are profoundly grateful for God's grace.	*Unity within community* Graduates worship in a local church community committed to making disciples, applying the truth of Scripture to everyday life, and striving for unity among God's diverse image-bearers.
Truth-bearers Graduates are equipped to articulate graciously and defend compellingly the Christian faith in all areas of life and culture.	*Abiding daily* Graduates abide in Christ, drawing their purpose, power, and guidance from the Holy Spirit through faithful engagement with and devotion to God's Word and prayer.	*God's kingdom ambassadors* Graduates love God and neighbor in unmistakable ways, proclaiming Christ's redeeming love in word and deed and serving with excellence in their relationships and vocational callings.

This work helped make visible a lot of assumptions and beliefs that would otherwise have remained invisible. Specifically, as we talked about the value of transformation, it immediately became clear that transformative learning takes place in two modalities: one that is instructional and intellectual, and the other that is participatory, experiential, and relational. If we wanted learning that resulted in outcomes like those we identified, it would require a learning spiral, in which instructional learning is followed by embodied practices. Our students would have to learn to *know* things and *do* things. Learning would have to move back and forth between the classroom and the settings of our students' daily lives. We strongly felt this spiral should take place in both the curriculum and the co-curriculum, not divided up between the two.

The Dean of Spiritual Development helped make this more visible by identifying many ways in which the cocurricular activities were already intersecting curricular learning:

1. We want graduates who abide in Christ, drawing their purpose, power, and guidance from the Holy Spirit through faithful engagement with and devotion to God's Word and prayer. There is a lot of content in our theology classes related to this, but it is substantially augmented by having hundreds of our students each year involved in spiritual direction. Spiritual direction is a place to process disconnects between what we know intellectually and what we experience in our hearts. For instance, a student may believe in God's patience and steadfast love but still fail to experience it. Of the 268 student prayer requests I received last week, one student wrote, "I need prayer for my insecurities because they are making me hate myself and bitter to people I love." This realization is a valuable step that opens up needs within the student's life and is a great contact point for spiritual direction. Offering spiritual direction to our undergraduates enhances the curriculum of graduate programs in spiritual formation by providing opportunities for supervised internships.

2. We want our graduates to ground their identities in Christ. For athletes, identity is a huge issue because performance has played such a central role in their lives. Their identities are prone to being attached to their athletics. They are their performance, their statistics, their wins and losses. Therefore, we encourage and equip coaches in their spiritual mentoring, athletic chapels, and FCA meetings, all of which help them understand the

complex world of identity and what identity in Christ means and looks like among our competing identities.

3. We want our graduates to be serving and carrying out ministry in their local contexts. A great training ground for this is the hands-on service and leadership experiences students have while serving in the various ministries on campus. They grapple with desires that sometimes flag and weaken when faced with overwhelming human need. It is an opportunity to discuss and educate the desires by reflecting on practice and to understand the theological process by which one grows in love and so can radiate Christ's love.

4. We want graduates to have faithful engagement with and devotion to God's Word and prayer. A guided prayer chapel called Fives, held at 5:00 p.m. twice a week, drew 960 students this past week who came to practice the biblical prayers of thanksgiving, confession, worship, intercession for self and others, and Scripture prayer. Students are also guided on what to do when these practices are difficult, unclear, or when they feel their energy flagging.

This short description helped make visible how much was already emerging from the conjunction of our curricular and cocurricular life. It also made clear to all of us that many of the qualities we wanted to cultivate in our graduates could only be achieved by the joint operation of all aspects of our institutional life. It also stimulated conversations about how this synergy could be enhanced.

Thinking about outcomes in terms of the qualities we wanted to see in our graduates also helped us think about classroom teaching. We realized we needed to actively work to close the gap between *theology learned* and *theology lived*. For example, theology learned tells us that we are made in the image of God, but theology lived expresses image-bearing in the daily life of students. In a culture obsessed with concerns about identity, they must find their identity in Christ—not only as a matter of theological truth but in their own psychological experience. The doctrine of adoption, for example, is an important theological truth, but to gain a new father in God and new brothers and sisters in the church has very tangible implications for the way a student answers the question, "Who am I?" Likewise, our theology must help us think about neighbor love in light of the pressing issues of our day. It must help us decide how we respect fellow image-bearers with whom we sharply disagree in matters of religion, politics, and community values. It must also help us understand what it means to bear the image of God even at the margins of life—its beginning and end. And our theological training must guide us in being salt and light, not just in theory or in critiques we offer of a naturalistic worldview, but in the way we actually live and act in our world. Our theology must help us speak the truth but also confront injustice, immorality, and idolatry. Our theology should guide the way we practice self-sacrificing love to friends and neighbors alike. Theology learned teaches that we are to love people from every nation, tribe, and tongue, but theology lived asks what that means when it comes to immigration policy. It also asks what that means when an undocumented immigrant comes to your university, church, or Bible study group. These are not questions with simple answers, but they are the questions our student will face upon graduation. We need to be intentional about preparing students to think through such questions. And faculty should be aware that these questions fit within the realm of classroom instruction. These questions demand integrative thinking that draws on both theology and a sound understanding of the world in which we live. We often deepen theology learned just by asking students what it would look like for theology to be lived.

Stating desired outcomes for our graduates stimulates thinking about ways in which assignments could be augmented to foster deeper learning. For example, the original list of desired outcomes for our graduates included graciously engaging with people who have varying political beliefs. Some professors have included an assignment in their classes that pairs students with their political opposites through a program called Unify America. The students are paired in a Zoom call with students from secular schools in other parts of the country, making this both an opportunity to learn to talk graciously about controversial issues and also an opportunity to be a kingdom ambassador. This classroom assignment can also stimulate interest in cocurricular projects. In our case, we have a club that stages discussions and structured debates with fellow believers who see things differently. We also partner with a group called Bridging the Gap, which helps us facilitate an intensive training in bridge building with students from a nearby secular liberal arts college. This program involves two weekend retreats, one on each campus, giving a very substantial encounter with those who see things differently. In these cases, classroom assignments can bridge seamlessly into cocurricular activities, which jointly contribute to the formation of our graduates.

We also used the desired qualities of our graduates to stimulate some creative brainstorming about the core curriculum and interdisciplinary classes. The exercise simply involved asking the question, "What if?" Here are some ideas that emerged:

- What if we cultivated a "faculty of the core," drawn from current faculty who *aspired* to teach CORE instead of being *required* to teach CORE?
- What if these faculty taught their classes together, not apart? What if they had total freedom to rearrange instructional hours and classroom settings?
- What if major class projects were designed to be shared between classes?
- What if faculty were trained in a cohort—participating together in paid summer sessions over a three-year period, learning the key questions in one another's disciplines, but also intentionally

training each other to see the theological/biblical issues that impinge on their own disciplines?

- What if they intentionally developed a shared vision of human flourishing and developed pedagogy that helped form students into flourishing human beings shaped into the likeness of Christ?
- What if the first two years of a Biola education were built around helping students identify the theology embedded in their ordinary life experiences—in things like movies, advertising, and the social media that bombards them?
- What if classes sometimes took place in a movie theater—with an hour-long discussion after watching the movie? What if they took place on a dorm floor or by the fire pit? What if they took place in a shopping mall or a coffee shop or at a Planned Parenthood Clinic or a Crisis Pregnancy Center?
- What if the class content were attached to Big Questions? For example, imagine a course examining the question, "Who am I?"
  - Theological material related to the image of God, the incarnation, and adoption would be included.
  - Psychological studies on personality theory, attachment theory, and identity formation would be included.
  - Literature, movies, plays, or art could all be included. (Attend a production of *Les Misérables* and discuss the question, "Who am I?")
- What if a yearlong seminar moved through a series of "big questions" such as, "Who am I?" to, "What makes life meaningful?" and, "What does it mean to be free?" and, "What is power?"
- What if we made these courses so good that no one would want to go to a community college for their first two years because they would feel like they were missing out on the essential core of a Biola education?

- What if we did not respond to ideas like this by saying, "It will never work!" but instead by asking, "What would we have to change to make this work?"

Conclusion

There is much more that can and should be done to operationalize the Christian formation of our graduates, but simply specifying our intentions and identifying ways in which we are currently working to achieve these outcomes in our graduates proved to be enormously helpful. The discussions that have been sparked by thinking through these outcomes have also been very fertile. It is easy and inspiring to talk about graduating students who "impact the world for Jesus Christ" (a phrase from our mission statement), but as someone pointed out in these conversations, we also need to equip our students to live as aliens and exiles in an increasingly hostile culture. It is valuable to equip our students to be leaders, but we also need to equip our students to be resilient and to know how to fail as well as succeed. All in all, it is apparent that developing a deep understanding of the sort of graduates an institution wants to produce is a very good way to own and implement the Christian mission of a university.

Questions

1. What are some of the qualities your institution most highly values in its graduates (a sample list was given on pp. 165–66)? Try to formulate this into a short description of what you would desire to see in a successful graduate several years after graduation.

2. How does your institution seek to form students into faithful followers of Christ? Do the curricular and cocurricular aspects of your

institution jointly share this responsibility, and if so, how do they coordinate their efforts?

3. If the goal of a Christian university is to graduate faithful Christian disciples, who is in charge of assessing this at your institution? How is this measured and celebrated?

GENERAL INDEX

SCRIPTURE INDEX